Hope the A

Hope the Archbishop

A Portrait

ROB MARSHALL

continuum
LONDON • NEW YORK

CONTINUUM
The Tower Building, 11 York Road, London SE1 7NX
15 East 26th Street, New York NY 10010

www.continuumbooks.com

First published 2004

British Library Cataloguing-in-Publication Data
A catalogue record for this book is available from the British Library.

ISBN: 0-8264-5420-8

Typeset by Kenneth Burnley, Wirral, Cheshire
Printed and bound in Great Britain by MPG Books Ltd, Bodmin, Cornwall

Contents

Introduction:
Creature of Habit

Two official portraits of David Michael Hope offer contrasting interpretations of one of the most popular and significant twentieth-century leaders of the Church of England. One was painted by Michael Noakes during Hope's time as Bishop of London, the other by Andrew Festing while he was Archbishop of York.

As ✠David Londin (a ✠ in front of a name denotes a bishop and the bishop's surname changes according to the See in his pastoral care) he is perceived as catholic, cosmopolitan, joyful, buoyant – a Yorkshireman unexpectedly relishing the challenge in the capital city. As ✠David Ebor, the brush has created a much more solemn, conservative, older, wiser Primate in his own land. People who have studied these paintings often plead for 'another David'. A visitor to Bishopthorpe Palace, his official residence in York, recently said of that painting: 'It's not really like him – I mean, he looks so serious. He is really so kind, so relaxed, one of us.'

This brief written portrait of David Hope, the son (a twin) of a Yorkshire builder, is a simple attempt to paint another picture: one that truly does capture his likeness. It is of necessity a partial, perhaps biased impression, born of 20 years at close quarters when I was Hope's press secretary. Hope's is a fascinating journey of steadfastness and courage but, above all, in secular times, faith.

I said at the outset that Hope is one of the most significant figures in the modern Church. If I were to point to one single thing that confirms me in this view, it is that, during the deeply divisive debate over the ordination of women to the priesthood, when the entire catholic wing of the Church could have split away, Hope became a pivotal figure. Through his wisdom, compassion, courage and deep faith, he helped the majority make the decision to stay. For him, whatever the issue, whatever the disagreement, the Church and its survival must come first.

But it is to the entirety of his time in the Church, the many key roles he has played, and to his many innate qualities, that we must look to paint a full portrait of Hope's significance, and to grasp his overall contribution. It has been his ability at all times to lead from the front, to command the respect of bishops, priests and laity, which has really established him as a remarkable modern church leader.

He is a devout priest who has always taken parish ministry very seriously. A man for whom mission – his own personal mission and that of the wider Church – is always the most important thing. A holy man. A loyal Anglican who, although a catholic, has remained totally committed to the Established Church. A man who, not because he wanted to but because it was asked of him, left parish ministry – which he loved – and applied his organizational, political and administrative skills to some of the most important roles within the Church.

Hope has lived a single, celibate life. He is married to the Church. He is happy living alone, and seems to relish the sense of inner peace which such a lifestyle has given him.

Like any single person, he has lonely times – when chewing over a major decision, a health matter, a dilemma or a problem. But he has solid reserves which always seem to see him through. Hope's sexuality has always fascinated people – much to his annoyance. It was as Bishop of London that he fell victim to a crude and disturbing whispering campaign that he was about to be 'outed' as gay. Hope challenged these rumours. He regarded the gossip as intimidatory and decided to confront those whom he knew were muttering in the corridors. He has always condemned those who victimize others on account of their sexuality and, as a celibate, said that his sexuality was a grey area which was of no concern to anyone but God and himself. The remarkable respect and love shown to him by the Church since that time has surprised even him.

The Archbishop is a slight figure. His handsome, characterful face is capable of pulling the most extraordinary expressions, betraying his innermost thoughts without him uttering a word. If Hope had had a *Spitting Image* puppet it would have spoken in the strongest of Yorkshire accents, been dressed in purple regalia and pulled very funny faces. He always looks smart: suits and slip-on shoes. He has large hands and neat hair. He watches his weight. He appears physically relaxed. His presence in a group or at a public gathering is reassuring and immediately obvious in a totally unassuming way. He is health-conscious. Some have suggested that he verges on being a hypochondriac.

Hope's working days begin early. He relishes that time when he can 'get on with things', when the house is silent, the world a quieter and more amiable place. Hope says Morning Prayer and Evening Prayer daily, and the regular rhythm of Bible readings, canticles and prayers are his chief source of inspiration. As Archbishop he has promulgated an early-morning Mass each day in the Bishopthorpe Palace chapel. It is frequently only attended by his chaplain, Mike Kavanagh, and himself. Breakfast follows early-morning Mass – just tea and toast. A bacon sandwich is enjoyed only on very special occasions. Each day is divided into three clearly defined parts: morning (administration, visits, interviews, meetings), afternoon (lunch, visits, interviews, meetings) and evenings (services, speeches, visits). Weekends are much the same, often with two key engagements in the diocese or province on Sundays.

His diary, published monthly, is circulated around the senior staff team. The workload is extraordinary and, apart from a three-week summer holiday, relentless. A study of 12 months of the diaries shows an average of 76 official engagements per month – and there are many other meetings, interviews and phone calls which are not listed.

Hope has attended many great banquets. He has eaten at the Mansion House, Buckingham Palace, Windsor Castle and Sandringham. But, left to his own devices, he is a man of simple tastes. His favourite food and drink are relatively straightforward. When he cooks for himself the emphasis is on plain, sometimes local, dishes. He likes beans on toast, adores Yorkshire fish and chips which he sometimes has as a treat. He stocks up on cheese, yoghurts, a bit of smoked salmon, sometimes a steak. He enjoys potatoes, is not keen on rice or pasta. He is dismissive of food which one might term 'modern' (sushi, curry – 'I'm not eating that stuff'). He is, as we shall see, a creature of habit. His love of wine and whisky is well known. To bring a busy day to a satisfactory conclusion, Hope begins with a glass of white wine and then moves on to a red. He ends with a whisky, and although people often buy him single malts, his favourite is Famous Grouse. He gives up alcohol completely in Lent and resorts to a late-night cup of Horlicks. ('I've just been to Tesco and bought the Horlicks' is an annual February lament.)

He remembers Jesus in the wilderness as he abstains from his late-night refreshment, until a glass of champagne on Easter Day brings the period of abstinence gratefully to an end. His mood lifts: 'It is lovely to relax at the end of the day with a glass of wine.' Hope's private sitting room in the palace on the bank of the River Ouse is unassumingly homely. He relaxes in his favourite reclining chair, feet up, and prefers a good CD to the TV which, as he flits from channel to channel with the remote control, is often accompanied by a totally hilarious and not very episcopal commentary: 'Look at her . . . what is he doing . . . honestly, there is nothing on . . . oh dear, they are at it again!' His significant CD collection reflects his knowledge of music, particularly choral works. When he was a victim of Loyd Grossman on *Through the Keyhole* (the TV programme in which a panel has to guess whose house the TV cameras are secretly visiting while the host is not present) it was the extensive selection of choral CDs that eventually gave the game away. Biographies dominate his non-theological bookshelf (he has a significant personal theological library in his study) and he has developed an increasing interest in the history of World War II. He reads widely, and avidly.

His bedroom is at one end of the guest wing in the palace, nearest the river. It is extremely basic and terribly dated in style. Until recently Hope always slept in a small, neatly-made single bed. He recalls his first night as the new resident of Bishopthorpe Palace vividly:

> I remember thinking, goodness me, is there really just me in this building? Anyway, I put the news on only to be told that someone had just escaped from the local prison and was on the prowl around York – police were looking for him, a convicted murderer – and I thought, good heavens! – if he gets in here that will be the end.

Hope said his Night Prayers and drifted off to sleep. But then, just a few minutes later, he was startled awake by multi-coloured flashing lights on the ceiling and walls of his ancient room, accompanied by the totally unexpected thumping sound of the Eurovision Song Contest winners, Abba, singing their hit single 'Money Money Money'. He thought he had already gone to hell ('What a din it was, what a carry on!'). But the lights and noise were the Saturday night Ouse disco boat, *The York*, that turns round alongside the palace. It was a feature of life as Primate of England which Hope had not expected.

The Archbishop of York's study is at the highest, furthest point from the official office entrance. Previous occupants have included Michael Ramsey, Donald Coggan, Stuart Blanch and John Habgood. Any contemporary visitor would climb a full set of 1970s-style wooden steps before following a long corridor into the Primate's office. Hope's desk, at which he spends hours, is always tidy but never free from piles of papers, letters, briefings, cuttings, books, magazines and official documents. He has his own computer in a far corner and a laptop which is used infrequently. Comfortable chairs ensure that guests are warmly greeted.

There are only two archbishops in the Church of England. Both have more than their fair share of church, regional, governmental and establishment business. This archbishop is fully proficient in e-mail and checks it regularly, but his handwriting is so difficult to read that he frequently cannot decipher it himself:

And, God has chosen ('Hold on, oh wait a minute'), has chosen ('Dear dear, I can't read what I have written'), God has chosen to reveal in the, in the, in the ('Oh goodness me I can't read my own writing').

Such a conversation on the telephone is always hilarious, the clear frustration over the illegibility rising, and then ending with 'I'll e-mail it to you as an attachment!'

He is in constant telephone contact with his advisers, senior staff, other bishops and Church of England officials. He has a mobile phone, but rarely turns it on, and only started text messaging in 2004. His life is organized through his electronic notebook diary in which are stored details of his main contacts.

Hope's attitude to the media is healthy, realistic and even support-ive. During his time as Bishop and Archbishop there have been very few journalists or media outlets which have managed to upset him in any lasting way. One or two have incurred his wrath fleetingly but, such is his tact, they are probably unaware of it to this day! Hope invariably reads *The Times*, and enjoys the *Yorkshire Evening Press* for local news. He reads the *Economist* and ploughs religiously through the *Sunday Times* and *Sunday Telegraph* ('Nothing to read at all . . . the fish and chips will be in them tomorrow'). He only rarely picks up a tabloid. Recently, when the soon-to-be unveiled Dean of York was staying as a guest at Bishopthorpe, Hope left him in the sitting room, advising him that the newspapers would arrive soon. For some reason *The Times* was not available that morning so the newsagent substituted a *Daily Mail*. 'There was the new Dean leafing through the *Daily Mail*. Goodness knows what he thought I read every day.'

But to suggest that Hope has ever been out of touch with reality would be ridiculous. His awareness of local news and some celebrity issues – grabbed from the local radio and newspapers – is often amazing. He enjoys car magazines too. While Hope respects the media, he has been extremely protective of his profile within it. He is very selective in what he does. For instance, he has never been interviewed live on the Radio 4 *Today* programme nor, despite over a hundred registered requests for the Archbishop to go on the *Breakfast with Frost* programme, has he ever graced that sofa: 'I am not rent-a-quote and I will only go on to say what I need to say at the right time.'

He tunes in, from time to time, to BBC Radio York or Humberside, for a local perspective, but his radio is generally set to Classic FM. He has no stomach for new, trendy comedy such as French and Saunders or Graham Norton. His hatred of what he describes as 'pure muck' on television is real. Hope enjoys *Songs of Praise* when he is not at a church on a Sunday evening, which is extraordinary, when you consider the huge number of hymns he hears and sings, and that the hymn-sandwich format is almost contrary to this sacramentalist. He probably enjoys the detachment from the occasion which the programme brings. He loves that very Yorkshire comedy *Last of the Summer Wine* in which his late friend Thora Hird starred until her death in 2003. Hope read the first lesson at her memorial service at Westminster Abbey.

Transport and buildings have interested Hope since his childhood. His father was a locally well-known builder in Wakefield and, as a tribute to him, he has incorporated a tiled roof in his personal coat of arms as Archbishop of York. Hope's fascination with buildings, structures, developments and refurbishment is always obvious and he is always keener to find out how the building was put together than what it cost or how the money was raised. He shows a similar interest in older buildings such as York Minster, his own cathedral. When visiting New York in 1999 he marvelled at the World Trade Center's twin towers and was appalled by the image of their collapse two years later – having eaten in the restaurant at the top of the southern tower. He watched his own retirement home being built and, even now, is keen to ensure that bricks and mortar are in perfect order. Hope is furious at what he sees as the lack of investment in the transport infrastructure by successive governments and classes it as a national disgrace.

He flies a good deal and is always pleased to 'get back down on to the ground'. He has covered hundreds of thousands of train miles on the East Coast line between York and London since becoming Archbishop of York and travels to London or beyond at least twice a week. He takes delight in his new-found ability to visit the website 'How's your train running?' and keeps up to date with the progress of southbound Glasgow and Edinburgh expresses on their way via York to London. In London, he always travels on the underground and only ever takes a taxi if he has to.

David Hope's one luxury in life is what he always refers to as 'my vehicle'. His passion for cars is amusing and, in many ways, totally out of character. He is a fast driver with a clean licence. The angels have guarded him against the rise of the speed camera. He is terribly impatient at the wheel – 'Get a move on . . . . Oh no, a tractor!' Since he became Bishop of Wakefield in 1985, he has always had an official car with the job. Although a driver (who usually doubles up as a gardener or handyman) has been provided (currently Gordon, whom he rates as excellent) Hope much prefers to drive himself, unless he is to drink at a function or if parking would be impossible when arriving at a royal or civic event. As Bishop of London his chauffeur, Fred, was indispensable because most of his engagements were in the City of London or around it and parking was virtually impossible. Hope believes the time is coming when bishops will not have chauffeurs. Having his own private car is his one indulgence, and few of them ever make it to Scotland twice for his annual holiday on the Isle of Skye. He likes to change them each June. From March onwards Hope is on the lookout – 'That's a nice model', 'I quite like the new Toyota', or 'I wouldn't mind a VW'.

Hope is an instinctive conservative. While, in his younger days, his father's influence may well have engrained within him an inner conservatism – 'My father always said that if you can't afford it, you can't have it' – he does not generally engage with politics or politicians. We will explore his attitude towards Blairism (if there is such a thing) and Thatcherism (he believes this certainly existed) later but it is clear that Hope has been generally suspicious of the long-term aims and objectives of New Labour. Ever since its landslide victory in 1997 he has had a rather heavy political heart. Tony Blair gained Hope's respect in the build-up to the 2003 Gulf War but he now believes that he was partly deceived, along with the majority of the population in the Western world. The failure to discover any weapons of mass destruction led Hope to revise his already hesitant support for the war, and to question the quality of American and British intelligence.

Hope hardly ever takes his seat in the House of Lords. He likes to approach all political issues from a theological standpoint. He does not see how Church and State can effectively engage politically without a clear, theological base and believes the tapestry, which is the Establishment, is being gently unstitched. Popular culture, as a whole, reflects the Godlessness and lack of spirituality in modern Britain, and this concerns him greatly.

Part of Hope's inner defence mechanism is to be private. Just about everyone I have spoken to about David Hope (and they number well over a hundred) makes some overt reference to the fact that they think they know him but cannot be sure. He gives of himself, reveals himself, to friends, but they are conscious that he always keeps something back. And while many would sympathize with him in this, on the grounds that some reserve is surely essential for self-preservation, there is an obvious danger of loneliness leading to unhappiness. This is something I believe Hope has fought with for some time – a battle he has latterly won. The problem is that Hope actually enjoys being alone. He relishes good company and a bit of gossip, but the nature of his vocation and his celibacy often combine to give the wrong impression of someone who is always keen to get back to the safe haven of his own space where he can be with God and 'let the rest of them get on with it'. In the last few years of his ministry this tendency to withdraw has diminished and he has enjoyed more social events and dinners. But it is a feature of his whole ministry that David Hope gives everything, and then withdraws – just as Jesus himself did, I suppose, to get away from the crowds.

Many believe Hope, in the nicest possible way, is prone to a little exaggeration. Tim Thornton, his Chaplain in Wakefield and London and now Bishop of Sherborne, lights up when he remembers those key phrases – 'I told him exactly what I thought. I said, now look here, don't you think you are getting away with this and that. I told him. I did. I left him in no doubt.' Thornton always interpreted this as 'I really wanted to tell him exactly what I thought. I wanted to say, now look here . . .' but he did not. He would be more gentle and tentative in such interviews and only firm on very rare occasions.

Hope is a creature of habit: the same routine, the same holiday, the same route, the same walk, the same meal, the same jumper. He likes to know when he's going, where he's going, who will be there and what time he can get away.

Within the confines of the Church of England, Hope is clearly regarded as a Tractarian Anglican who has stayed within his church despite the momentous decision, in 1995, to ordain women to the ministerial priesthood. He continues to disagree fundamentally with this move, not because he dislikes or disapproves of women but because such a unilateral action in the context of worldwide Christendom seemed wrong. He also points to the fact that the advent of women priests has not led to a radical upturn in either attendance or morale.

Hope has immense authority at the altar. Simplicity, grace and presence are key words which summarize his liturgical presence. He transcends any opposition to his remaining in a church from which many fled in fear of schism and collapse. Hope consecrates bishops and ordains deacons with the same simplicity and authority. He is steeped in scripture (he always uses a biblical text as the foundation for his preaching) and enjoys reading the teachings of the early desert Fathers who have inspired and motivated him in his own life and ministry. But as hundreds of priests and laity left the Church of England, either before, at the time, or just after 1995, Hope has remained and endured, at times with great pain and a sense of bereavement.

Hope loves the Church of England, but he is fearful about the current financial climate and recognizes the difficulties it faces: rationalization, shrinkage, reduced impact and influence. Hope prays this through. The devotion and work of the laity is a source of endless encouragement to him; the hard work and diligence of many priests and bishops generally inspires him. He is also much loved by the various Anglican religious communities around Britain, many of which enjoy links with him. But he laments the drift which unilateralism has brought about and is sceptical (though not unenthusiastic) about ecumenism. Many believe that if the ordination of women had come about earlier, before he became a bishop, David Hope would have moved on somewhere else – but where to is uncertain. Rowan Williams draws attention to David Hope's exposure to Eastern Christianity, suggesting that he does not personally regard David as a 'Papalist'. Hope recognizes authority and responds to it; the Archbishop of Canterbury is right. The paradox of Hope is that, while Anglicanism has shifted its ground in a dramatic way, Hope could not have found solace in either the Roman Catholic or Orthodox Churches without seriously lamenting his own church.

In his final role as Vicar of St Margaret's, Ilkley (fulfilling a desire to end where it all began), Hope may well be able to gain a sense of perspective after a roller-coaster ride as a theological college principal, Bishop of Wakefield, Bishop of London and Archbishop of York. He has seen massive change in both the Church and the world. He has remained faithful and diligent to God's calling; but it has not always been easy.

1

Small Builder

David used to take services for the family. We all used to sit in the attic room and he would be the vicar. We used to have hymns and he would preach. Yes, at 11 he would preach to us all. And, believe it or not, he had a collection!

(Anne Hope)

Wakefield is Yorkshire through and through, and so is its son, David Hope. The town, ten miles south of Leeds in the Calder Valley, grew rich in the eighteenth century as the centre of the Yorkshire textile trade, and in the nineteenth from the fruits of the industrial revolution – when coalmines replaced the trade in cloth from this inland port on the River Calder.

Wakefield was the county town of the old West Riding of Yorkshire, and still has the warm, settled, county feel that Hope associated with it during his childhood. Today it is a post-industrial place, its coal pits exhausted and its mining heritage recalled only in the National Coal Mining Museum, the former Caphouse colliery in which tourists can now travel underground for a sanitized taste of life at the coal face.

One constant throughout the town's history has been its fourteenth-century Cathedral Church of All Saints, whose 75-metre (247-feet) spire dominates the city centre. The cathedral has been central in David Hope's life as well. At the age of ten he was a chorister here; 35 years later he would return as its Bishop.

Hope sees himself as being hewn from dependable Yorkshire stock: 'We were comfortable,' he says, 'solid, predictable I suppose. But my

1

family gave me a firm grounding and laid foundations which were to see me through my life and my ministry. They were not exceptional, but they were fine.' David's father – Jack Hope – took on the family building firm, founded by his father, and married Florence Rhodes, who was born into a typically large Yorkshire family in the nearby town of Pontefract – the only girl alongside five boys. She was a schoolteacher. The Hope family home was at 141 Thornes Lane from where Jack also ran his building firm. He employed up to 16 men and the demands of the small business dominated much of his life.

Florence was unconventional in that she did not settle down as an ordinary Yorkshire housewife, but continued with her career. She rode a motorcycle to school every morning, and David still has a picture of his mother on the bike, and chuckles over it. She taught at All Saints, Pontefract and, according to those who knew her, enjoyed her work enormously.

The Second World War was raging when David and his twin sister Anne were born. They came forth on a dark Sunday evening on 14 April 1940 at the home, in Millthorpe Lane, of the local midwife, Nurse Bailey. The nurse brought many Yorkshire children into the world. David Hope's birth was a difficult one, and he tells of it with relish and a twinkle in the eye:

> The doctors were pretty worried: there had been some kind of complication and they decided that it would be better to be safe than sorry so they called in the vicar to baptize me just in case. Everyone was in quite a state when he came round and, when he asked my mother for something to put the water in, all she could find was a Yorkshire pudding tin. So I was baptized from that – quite appropriate really.

Hope laughs: 'It was Yorkshire tap water too!'

It would be understandable if war had cast a shadow over Hope's early childhood. Just 40 miles away, the important port of Hull was being bombed beyond recognition. Indeed, Hope's earliest memories are of the war. Yet the portrait you gather from those memories is of a warm, close family life cradled in a safe, nurturing community. Shielded from the horrors, his recollections are humorous.

To eke out meagre wartime and post-war rations, Hope's father teamed up with neighbours and kept pigs: 'They bought three pigs,' Hope recalls,

> . . . and I can remember some of the laughs which came – having pigs in the house. They had to register them. They used to be allowed to wander everywhere around the yard before they were put back into the pigsty. I can remember going next door and mixing the feed. They would be slaughtered just before Christmas and then I have strong recollections of my mother rendering down the fat. It was precious for cooking. A chap from a local company used to come and salt the hams and they were hung in the attic. Every three weeks he would come and stick a needle up the back of the hams to see if they had cured.

Then there was Hope's Uncle Willie, one of his mother's five brothers, who was managing director of Muscrofts, a local brewery. During the war, Willie was the 'magician' who could produce goods which no one else could get their hands on: 'On firework night, for instance, my mother would send us over to Uncle Willie's to get some fireworks, and at Christmas he could get boxes of liquorice allsorts.'

David and Anne would travel to Pontefract every Saturday, a trip that always included a visit to the market tripe stall to enjoy the wonderful delicacy of uncooked honeycomb tripe soaked in salt and vinegar! 'I used to enjoy it but I couldn't stomach the thought of it right now!'

Wakefield is Hope's home. 'It has its own feel,' he says. It was, and is, his place of belonging. A place where he knew almost everyone and almost everyone knew him. In his childhood landscape, two little places loomed large – the corner shop where he and Anne would run errands for their mother, and the barber's:

> I used to go to Cyril Hudson's to have my hair cut and you certainly did learn about life in there. In fact my mother stopped me going because there were too many juicy stories being told, I can tell you. The shop always smelt of burnt hair. I can still smell it now. When he had cut your hair he would singe it – to finish it off. So there was always this terrible smell!

To that young boy with his vivid senses, Wakefield's seasons were much more clearly defined than he finds them today. 'It was certainly colder, warmer, frostier, depending on the season . . . and I can remember the smog, the fog; it left you feeling moist, damp around your face.'

David and Anne started at Gaskill's School on Thornes Road – not far from the family home. It had just two teachers, Miss Selley and Miss Norris, and the twins always went on a three-wheeled tandem. There was often a fight as to who would be the driver. 'We would take it in turns,' concedes David. There was a bomb shelter in the school, and an air-raid practice resulted in he and Anne trying to get the tandem in the shelter so that it did not get damaged. The tandem got stuck, they were in trouble and teachers banned it. At Christmas, the children took ingredients (2oz of sugar or flour) and Miss Selley would bake shortbread as a treat. 'I can remember making decorated Christmas puddings with arms – little people Christmas puddings. It was fun.' He enjoyed his early days, even those little compulsory bottles of milk he was forced to drink: 'Oh, it was awful in the summer when it got hot and the cream turned. Terrible. But we still drank it!' Anne, a physiotherapist, is now married to Peter Westwood, a former superintendent in the West Yorkshire police force. They have two children, Andrew and Suzanne. 'We had a great childhood really, we were very different, despite being twins. We fought and had arguments like all brothers and sisters do, but generally we got on well.'

Anne was the extrovert. She loved going out to play with the neighbourhood children, David was more withdrawn and serious. 'He would come out and play sometimes but if he did he was the organizer: he would always sit on the sidelines and we did what he said, believe it or not! I would come in filthy from playing and David would be reading books, always studying and spending more time with the adults. Not in a negative kind of way – it was just David, more serious and grown-up for his age.'

The effect of the building firm being run from home imposed itself on the twins: 'I remember the scaffolding, the ladders and the equipment dad used,' says Anne. 'During the holidays dad would sometimes take us on to a building site and we loved it. He would have us mixing the concrete and helping out, which was great at our age!' Mr Hope worked with several other craftsmen including the plasterer

Arthur Longbottom and joiner Arthur Bell, also the local undertaker. It was a classic Yorkshire set-up.

From Gaskill's, David progressed to St James's Junior School, underneath the arches in Thornes Lane. Mr Pattinson was the head teacher. Assemblies consisted of a hymn (usually 'New Every Morning'), a reading and a prayer – the Morning Collect was always said ('Almighty God, we thank thee that thou hast brought us safely to the beginning of this day'). 'The notices were given out and then he got the cane out. When that happened you knew school had started.'

David won a Choral Scholarship to Queen Elizabeth Grammar School for boys at the age of ten – a major event in his early development. Apparently, he had a wonderful voice and was an exceptional choirboy. He was as naughty as the rest of them on occasions but his seat in the choir stalls gave the future archbishop a unique view of the Church at worship in just about every conceivable situation – ordinary services, special occasions, civic and royal events. He would later recall his greatest fear as a child:

> Believe it or not, we always had the threat of a caning hanging over us if ever we were said to have been talking during the sermon or doing anything naughty like that. In those days it could mean lining up in the vestry for a caning but luckily it didn't come to that for me. Once, the provost warned me and another choirboy about eating fish and chips in a main street so after that I ate them in a side street!

Anne remembers her brother as a chorister: 'I have never really sat with David in church – even when we were young. He was always up there, in the choir stalls, even from an early age. My cousin Muriel used to take us to the cathedral and I would always go to the 11am service. David enjoyed the choir.' Anne can remember the first time it dawned on her that David might be destined for ministry in the Church. The young boy was so caught up in the liturgy and majesty of what went on at the cathedral that, while other children would enjoy playing post offices or shops, Hope 'played churches'. He would frequently gather his two grandmas, who had come to live with the family, his parents, Anne and anyone else he could lay his 11-year-old hands on to come to his church in the attic:

He used to take services for the family. He must have been keen when I think about it. We all used to sit in the room and David would be the vicar. We used to have hymns and he would preach. Yes, at 11 he would preach to us all. And, believe it or not, he had a collection! My mother made sure he gave it to the Provost.

As a result of these early celebrations in the Hope attic Anne can trace her family's inevitable belief that David would enter the Church. He was dedicated, always committed, devout and faithful. David was close to his grandmothers. Anne recalls that, in the winter,

they were always ill in bed with bronchitis. David used to go upstairs and speak to Grandma Hope and Grandma Rhodes. He was the bee's knees. He always used to come downstairs with some cash in his hand saying that he had had his palm crossed with silver –meaning that he had been given a treat – and Mum always insisted that he shared it with me even though I hadn't done a thing!

Queen Elizabeth Grammar School is today rightly proud of its former pupil. It still has a fine reputation within the West Yorkshire area and the scholarship provided David with a solid educational foundation – though, as a choirboy, it was difficult at times in a school with a strong rugby and football tradition. 'It was OK. I enjoyed school on the whole. I particularly enjoyed the sixth form.' Hope relished the fact that by then he was treated more as a student than a schoolchild. Not that there is any suggestion he was ever bullied, but as a theological, musical, non-sporty boy he found the less-regimented life in the sixth form more amenable.

The family always had a car of some description. David's love of four wheels surely dates back to this. He has an early memory of his father's building van, taking the family on a trip to Bramham Park, a Queen Anne mansion and gardens at Wetherby. They also had a Jeep for a time and a trip to the coast at Flamborough flashes in front of David's eyes:

I loved Flamborough from an early age. A very special, open place. We once went on a trip there in this Jeep thing and I sat in the back with Anne, Mum and Dad in the front. The funny thing is my Mum wanted to 'pay a call' every so often during that trip, much to my Dad's frustration: because of the noise, Mum had to signal whenever she needed a toilet stop and so she held up a white handkerchief.

Another vivid early memory, and one which links family life with Hope's growing sense of vocation, was the Coronation of Queen Elizabeth II on 2 June 1953.

I recall our ten-inch black and white television set which had been delivered and set up just in time for the ceremony. We were all immensely excited. Preparations had been going on for some time. Our front room had been rearranged cinema-style so that we could fit a few of the neighbours as well as other family and friends into the room. It was to be an all-day session. After all, we had seen nothing like it before – this new wonder of television – and the coronation of Her Majesty Queen Elizabeth II.

The ceremony was breathtaking. One of the main highlights was the moment of the anointing as the canopy was placed over Her Majesty, and the Archbishop of Canterbury took the Holy Oil, anointing her as kings and priests and prophets had been long ago and down the ages. It was a truly awesome and potent sign amidst all the pageantry and splendour of the day that all power comes from God and all who exercise earthly power do so as sacred trust.

Hope always speaks affectionately of the Queen. Whenever he has met her, at an official function or in more relaxed circumstances, his respect and admiration for a woman of immense integrity, service and faith is obvious.

During those early, formative years, it was the rhythm and life of Wakefield Cathedral which made the greatest impression on David Hope. As a chorister he had seen it all – the big festivals, the cold Sunday mornings, the special occasions. He understood at an early age what the dean did, who the bishop was, what the significance was of certain county, city and community events, and he loved it:

The cathedral, through being there and being part of the whole thing, did make an impression on me. Those great feast days, the organ, the colour, and the event. The vestments, all the lot of it.

You got caught up in it. It was lovely really. Apart from getting your legs slapped for messing about under the pews of course. I remembered all of that the day I became Bishop.

I suppose my first sense of vocation was in those early years. There was an incipient vocation – there were others in the choir, who were serving, who went on to be priests and bishops. Alan Chesters, former Bishop of Blackburn, was another of that generation. I never really, to be honest, thought of anything else.

Perhaps because the life of the Church became such an integral part of Hope's own life at such an early age, he cannot identify any one moment of epiphany at which it became clear to him that God was calling him into the Church. 'I had no Damascus road experience, I couldn't point to the moment when the Lord seized me. It's been much more of an unconscious emergence.'

David Hope's father died in 1981, but his mother was to live to see her son become Bishop of Wakefield in 1985.

Yes, it was really wonderful that she was able to be present in Wakefield Cathedral to see me become Bishop after all those years of going there as a family in those early days.

Anne remembers their mother's excitement when she heard that David was in line for the bishopric in Wakefield: 'It was mooted in the *Yorkshire Post* for some months. She saw the report and rang me up. She had almost stopped smoking, but when she saw David's name as an almost certainty for Wakefield she went out and bought a packet of cigarettes!'

Anne is in no doubt that David was the favourite of the twins but for all the right reasons.

Yes, David was always the favourite – it was a very busy household, there was a lot going on with two grandmothers living with us. I never really thought of it at the time but he was the most homely, and the older ones liked that. He is more like our mother than our Dad really, in his ways and nature, but the building background is still there in his blood. He still loves the fact that Father ran the building firm.

Hope is incredibly proud of his father, a fact reflected in his inclusion of a tiled roof as part of his coat of arms as Archbishop of York.

Hope completed his education with good grades, and was set to move away from home to university for the first time. Theology seemed the best and most appropriate option. Wakefield had set him up 'good and proper'; now he would test his growing sense of vocation in the wider world.

2

Priest

I had a friend who had gone to be David Hope's curate in Warrington . . . I heard quite a bit about David the vicar through [him]. I had an early impression of a devout priest who took parish ministry very seriously.

(Rowan Williams)

David Hope's wish to return to parish ministry in Ilkley after his retirement as Archbishop of York reminds us of his vocation: as a priest in the Church of God. To return to his roots in this way will take him a world away from the role he played from 1995 to 2004 as, to give him his full title, the Most Reverend and Right Honourable the Lord Archbishop of York. He has never lost sight of his priestly role: Hope the priest is indeed Hope the man.

As he matured from the chorister into the theology student, his almost instinctive sense of vocation grew with him. Hope chose the University of Nottingham to study theology. It was here that his spiritual life and his awareness of his calling developed and matured. Interestingly, theology was not his first choice of subject.

I was going to read History, but when I got there for the interview I happened to meet Alan Richardson, who was then Professor of Theology, and he said, 'Why don't you read Theology instead?', so I thought about it, and decided I would. At various points of my life I've gone down a certain path because of one individual or other whom I have met, and whose advice has had a profound effect on the way my life has moved.

Hope remembers the move away from home:

I stayed in digs from year one and it was the first time I had lived on my own. You got on with it, without thinking about it. I shared a room with another student, a physicist. I had quite a number of close friends and we used to go to Yates's Wine Lodge most weeks for a tipple. Life was different. It was fun.

I sang in the university choir and got quite involved in the students' union – those Rag Week raids on Mansfield were memorable!

The course itself was a standard university degree in Theology.

One had to do Greek and Hebrew. Also texts, which we had to study in detail. There was exegesis as well. After the third year I specialized in Early Church History and it was then that I read all the letters of Cyprian of Carthage, from the third century, in Latin. I suppose this was the moment when the teaching of the Fathers became very important to me.

The Fathers inspire us. There was the revolt against too close an accommodation with the state following the Settlement of Constantine. It was a very extremist, in some ways puritanical movement which went into the desert. It was a movement of protest for the things of God. They saw the world as disastrous. The world, the way it was going, was a shipwreck. As the Fathers saw it, they were seeking to rescue the world from disaster. Their sayings are very pithy. Sometimes mad. But always with a sharp grain of truth about the reality of life and living. Isaac the Syrian is a favourite – he speaks about diving deep within yourself to discover the rungs by which you will ascend. Dive deep into yourself and there you will discover the treasure house of heaven.

Hope urges the Church in the twenty-first century to heed the teaching of the Fathers.

Particularly at Easter, it is good to remember their contribution. Their teachings speak loudly to us. For example, Cyril of Jerusalem, in the very place where Jesus was crucified, would sit in the church each evening and teach about what had happened. He would explain the mysteries of the faith. You have the catechetical lectures beforehand. There are lessons to be learned, bearing in mind the paucity and scarcity of teaching about the fundamentals of the Christian faith.

Hope's studies further strengthened his sense of vocation, and after speaking to the Bishop of Wakefield's representative with special responsibility for vocations, and then to the Bishop himself, David Hope took the next step along the road to priesthood.

I went to St John's Durham for my selection conference. I can remember going out to the pub late one night and as we approached the college one of the selectors saw us. I thought, 'Good heavens, that's kyboshed it.' But I went through the process and found out that I had succeeded in going through to ordination. Bishop John Ramsbottam told me that I had been recommended for training and, with the Nottingham course still going ahead full steam, I had to put my mind to which theological college I should go to.

Father Plumbridge, who had taught me Latin at school and who was another huge influence, said that there was only one place for me to go: St Stephen's House, Oxford, and so it was. I'd been brought up and formed very strongly in the Anglican Catholic tradition, the Tractarian tradition. It wasn't any fancified religion, just good northern straight-down-the-line Anglo-Catholicism; no bells and smells nonsense. That's where I was formed and where I belonged, and St Stephen's was in that tradition.

Hope arrived in Oxford in 1962, when the 1960s were beginning to swing.

I did three years at Oxford so that I could do some research. I got a state studentship to do a DPhil. at Linacre College. I had to do about six papers for the general ordination exam, which qualified me for ordination, and I could spend the rest of the time doing research, which I loved.

St Stephen's House was a relatively strict place and you had to accept the regime as it was. We were summoned by bells. We began each day with Meditation followed by Morning Prayer and Mass. That was all before breakfast. Then the courses began and I would go to the university library. Lunch and the afternoon were followed by Evensong and supper and there were even lectures in the evening. During the day there was the lesser silence which meant that at lunchtime and after Evensong there was no unnecessary talking. It was quasi-monastic. At 10pm there were Night Prayers followed by 20 minutes of silence. We finished with the Grace at 10.20 and then the Greater Silence started and you could not leave the college or talk until breakfast the next morning. Wednesday was a free night and Sunday too, but otherwise it was a strict regime.

People were committed to this Rule of Life. There were fun times and relaxation too. Holy Week was a very special time. Pantomime time was always spectacular – we put on 'Mother Goose' and 'Jack and the Beanstalk'!

I think the media preoccupation with a camp tradition of single men at St Stephen's is overdone and certainly it was no more or no less evident than at other institutions of its kind.

Because of its discipline and routine, I felt that I was given a structure to my spiritual life which provided me well for the future. I certainly regret some modern trends where the word 'discipline' does not feature. Discipline has not been incorporated in an imaginative way into some of the courses. The key word here is 'formation' – fundamental in any Anglican Catholic structure or ministry. These colleges really did form priests. Today, we hear about training and not much about formation. That is what is missing.

Hope's DPhil. was an exciting project for him.

In simple terms, it was a study which took me to the Verona Library, the Vatican Library and the National Library in Paris. It was thought that the Roman Liturgy, the worship of the Western Church, emerged first of all in the Leonine Sacramentary. Then there followed the Gelasien Sacramentary and then the Gregorian Sacramentary. That was the thinking. But it is clear that the

Leonine Sacramentary was never, in fact, used as a public Mass book at all. However, on some of the great feast days, such as St Peter and St Paul, you find not one Collect of the Day, but up to 28 – and many of them dependent on each other. You will see echoes of the sermons in the prayers of Leo and echoes of the prayers in the sermons. Which came first? Which influenced the other? It is clear by the same token that Gelasius and Pope Verglius also contributed to prayers in that book. So maybe the Leonine Sacramentary was not written by Leo at all but was instead a compendium of different prayers and resources. I have no doubt that it was a Papal Book. It was at a time that the liturgy was not fixed. The pope might just compose a Collect and then look back and say: 'Shall I use the one I used last year or shall I vary it?' The Leonine Sacramentary is in the Verona Library, which is strange in itself, so there are some intriguing questions about the origins of this book which fascinate me even today.

The study meant that I had to look clearly at evidence to check out the veracity of what was being said. To this day I am careful about accepting what people *say* that people said. Sifting evidence carefully is important.

Hope was eventually chosen to serve his title (become a curate) in Tuebrook, Liverpool, a familiar training ground for deacons from St Stephen's House.

I was told that that is where I should go by my theological college and so I went. There was none of this ridiculous computer-dating nonsense – matching people up and all of that. That was the Church into which I was ordained. Clifford Martin was Bishop of Liverpool at the time. I did go and have a look at the parish over a weekend and thought how right it seemed and so, yes, I was ordained in Liverpool Cathedral by Bishop Stuart Blanch.

Anne Hope remembers attending. What Hope's proud family cannot have had any inkling of as they sat in the pews that day was that Blanch would soon be promoted to be Archbishop of York and that his young ordinand would one day follow him: 'It was a bit like a degree ceremony really,' says Anne. 'All of us attending, wearing our best clothes. He had reached the next stage of his career. I never really felt it was odd when I saw him in a collar. I trained as a physiotherapist and had to wear a uniform and my husband Peter was in the police force so he had a uniform too. The dog collar was David's uniform for the job.'

And then it was off to do what God had called him to do. After time in Nottingham and Oxford, Hope must have found the down-to-earth honesty and fun of the Merseyside people rather a contrast to university life. Hope was in Tuebrook between 1965 and 1967.

In those days you couldn't be choosy. I started in digs in Liverpool at £500 per year. There was no house for the curate. I sent my washing back to my Mother and my Dad would help me out financially. There is always something inescapably significant for me personally about Liverpool. When the House of Bishops goes back there every year I can't help but think that this is where it began.

Hope's vicar in Liverpool was Frank Sampson – locally known as Sammy – a good old-fashioned Anglo-Catholic priest. Hope's fellow curate was David Diamond, a well-known character in the Anglican Catholic movement, mainly because of his amazing work with young people in the south London suburb of Deptford. Father Samson, Father Diamond and Hope proved to be an excellent, effective team.

At the funeral of David Diamond, in September 1998, Hope drew on his earlier experiences when in Liverpool:

St John's Hall, Tuebrook, in the early 1960s, was a seething mass of young people, not least on a Friday night. It was the time when Liverpool's Cavern Club [where the Beatles famously performed] was thriving. I can remember one such night very well, when the ever-popular Wild Wild Clubs were to be performing. It was a holy day of obligation, so, of course, no Mass: no dance. We scraped through the Mass, and there were literally scores of girls and boys who would never in the ordinary course of events have dreamed of entering a church building. Then, on entering the youth club, Father Diamond said to me: 'Oh Farv, we're short of helpers tonight, would you please stand at the emergency door?' What he'd omitted to tell me was that a marauding gang was expected and their accomplices were to let them in through the emergency door. He was always well informed. He knew the buzz. We survived the night – but only just.

There was another important aspect of David Diamond which rubbed off on Hope when they were curates:

He was no party man. He was not much into committees and groups and so much of that which consumes time and energy in the Church today. Rather, for him, time and energy were to be spent in the service of his people, in the living of that basic incarnational principle in and among the people he served.

Hope spent 1967–1968 in Romania (more of which in the next chapter) then returned to Tuebrook for a couple of years before being appointed Vicar of St Andrew's, Orford in Warrington in 1970. He was to serve four years in the parish. Hope says:

These days you would call Orford an Urban Priority Area – it is an estate on the northern edge of Warrington. It had been a daughter church and then became a parish in its own right and a new church was built. It was busy; the basic bread and butter of parish life was demanding. We had 50 house Communions every month, four funerals a week, weddings most Saturdays. It was strong on young people, there was a good church school, an old people's club and bingo. It was a lively, active parish. We used to take three or four buses to Blackpool lights every year.

Hope also lived in a vicarage for the first time. It was a fairly modern house, next door to the parish church, and on Mondays he would have an office evening when local people could come and meet him.

By the time he left Orford, Hope had spent four years diligently carrying out the everyday work of a parish priest. He had little thought of the church hierarchy of which he was on a lowly rung, or indeed of the Church outside the areas in which he carried out his pastoral duties. London was for now a distant, almost completely unknown place. 'I didn't go there very often. Certainly not for church events. London didn't figure. It wasn't on the radar.' Not for now, anyway.

It was during this time that Rowan Williams first came across his future colleague.

I had a friend who had gone to be David Hope's curate in Warrington – a chap called John Saywood, who has since joined the Roman Catholic Church. Consequently, I heard quite a bit about David the vicar through John. I had an early impression of a devout priest who took parish ministry very seriously.

Hope's work and gifts, unbeknown to him, were being noticed, in London and elsewhere. He had an inherent quality of priesthood about him and had quickly adapted to his liturgical duties. At the altar Hope did things simply and clearly but with authority. He was bright, confident, attractive and, most important of all within the Catholic movement, a loyal Anglican who recognized the strength of the Established Church and was committed to the Tractarian tradition. Hope was serious, without taking himself too seriously. He was a people man; bright but with a common touch; academic, with a strong commitment to parochial ministry and mission. He liked being with and alongside the Church at work and despised red tape, bureaucracy and politics. So perhaps, it was being mentioned in the Church's corridors of power, it was time to test his skills in a higher post?

Indeed it was, and his old college was about to call him to sort it out from top to bottom. 'I was never aware that my name was being mentioned for other things,' says Hope today.

It honestly never crossed my mind. I suddenly received a letter from Eric Kemp, then Dean of Worcester, asking me to go and meet the governing body of St Stephen's House and that was my first realization that my name was around for other things. I was eventually offered the job as Principal of St Stephen's, and Stuart Blanch – then Bishop of Liverpool in whose diocese I was working – was chair of the evangelical college Wycliffe Hall. He said that there would need to be a collaboration between St Stephen's and Wycliffe, and he was very encouraging. He was hesitant about me going but in the end he decided I ought to.

It was a most significant development for David Hope, because this was his first step away from a parish and, apart from his two years in Romania, away from the north, where he has always felt most at home. Almost, one senses, against his wishes, the Church was calling him to help in ways which took him away from his reasons for becoming one of its priests. But who was he to resist the call?

3

Securitate and Staggers

David . . . did tremendous things at St Stephen's House and
when he became Bishop of Wakefield I had no doubt that he
would go on in the Church.

(Robert Runcie)

David Hope's posting to Bucharest, Romania, as Chaplain to the
Church of the Resurrection, is an early instance of his talents recom-
mending him to his superiors. He was seen as a promising curate who
might be stretched in an environment which would be less familiar to
him than that of the north of England.

His arrival coincided with the start of the despotic regime of
Nicolae Ceausescu in 1967. The communists, with the protection of
Soviet troops, had taken control of the country in 1947, forcing the
monarch, King Michael, to give up his throne and killing or impris-
oning political opponents. Ceausescu became head of state at a time
when opposition to Soviet interference was strong, and his national-
ist stance was popular. His denunciation of the 1968 Soviet invasion
of Czechoslovakia and a brief relaxation of internal repression
helped give him a positive image both at home and in the West.
However, his regime became more and more oppressive and resulted
in grotesque violations of human rights. His secret police, the
Securitate, were feared, and with good reason. Caeusescu was finally
swept from power in 1989, and executed. Amid violence and
confusion an impromptu governing coalition, the National
Salvation Front, installed itself and proclaimed the restoration of
democracy.

In England, Hope followed events avidly. He has an abiding interest in Romania: he still speaks the language with great confidence, and his interest in, and concern for, the people remains as strong today as it was then. He has continued to support Romanian orphanage projects and has returned to the country regularly.

In 2004, David Hope took a party of 80 pilgrims to Romania to explore the formation of the early Church in Europe. Accompanying him on the journey, we were able to see the excitement and challenges which this country had offered Hope as a young priest. The role he was called upon to fulfil in Romania was a most unusual one.

The first Anglican Chaplain was posted to Romania as early as 1868. Apart from two periods – during World War II and following the 1989 revolution – the Anglican Church has remained open for services. It is the only East European Anglican Church to have functioned throughout the communist era. The Chaplain has semi-diplomatic status and has limited use of the diplomatic bag for incoming and outgoing mail. He is also *de facto* Chaplain to the British Embassy. The congregation in Bucharest is made up of expatriates – long-term residents, transitory embassy employees, business people and teachers. Services, all conducted in English, are held every Sunday morning.

Hope's time as a Chaplain in Romania had a profound effect on him. For the first time he savoured a culture and a people far removed from Yorkshire, or the middle England of the Church. Perhaps it has enabled him to regard the life and decision-making processes of the Church of England with a greater degree of objectivity.

Hope is clear that the Romania of Cauceseau was a very grim place. 'You never quite knew what was going to happen next, where people disappeared to; there was real fear, uncertainty, evil. You really couldn't trust anybody, not even within the Church.'

He had a small, spartan room in Bucharest; there was just a table, a bed, a chair, and little else but the few books he had brought with him. 'I really had to exist with the minimum but in a way it was quite invigorating – there was a sense of freedom in the context of all that control and fear – life was there to be lived.'

Hope soon established a pattern to his working day: rising early to pray before spending time getting to know the local community, making friends with English speakers and non-English speakers alike.

He gave an insight into how strongly he feels for Romania in a sermon at St Martin in the Fields on 1 February 1992, following a return visit:

I have to say that I was both shocked and saddened at the state of the capital city, Bucharest – a fine and noble city which, even in the short time I had been there, I had come to know well and hold in great affection. The despoliation of the Ceausescu regime was evident in almost every street. Yet even amid such outward and visible devastation and destruction, I was immensely encouraged and heartened by the indomitable spirit of the people. We rejoice at the collapse of tyranny and fear, but a price has been paid and continues to be paid by those who have endured them and who are now freed from them.

He was also keen on developing ecumenical contacts with the local Orthodox community, and it was here that he first experienced the paradox of Orthodox liturgy, its formality and informality, which he found so appealing: 'The whole of life was there: people standing, waiting, looking, hugging: the icons, bread and wine, the rich symbolism and diversity. It made life extremely interesting and there was a real sense of drama and expectation.'

It was after Hope was made Bishop of London in 1991 that he became more acutely aware of the problems facing many of the children and young people of Romania.

I became involved with the charity Children in Distress and went out to bless the site at Cernavoda where the first children's hospice would be built on the Danube Delta. I remained in touch with the charity. They had an annual service which I attended. I wanted to work as much as possible with the Orthodox Church so that we had proper links in Romania. I also tried to help the Christian Children's Fund by opening their new centre in Cluj in central Romania. The children of Romania are still facing abandonment – some have no parents or families – and the challenge is to get them back into real homes, foster homes. Health care and diet were also key issues.

I sat with David Hope as he reflected, during the 2004 pilgrimage, on the unfolding situation in Romania. Since the fall of communism the life of the Romanian people has changed significantly. The country has recently become a member of NATO and is hopeful of EU membership in 2007. The standard of living has increased significantly: whereas Western goods used to be scarce and expensive they are now widely available at reasonable prices.

We were sitting in the lobby of a hotel in the town of Gura Humorului, where a conference on child protection in Romania was taking place: 'The future for the children of this country has improved since the revolution but there is still a long way to go and too many children are in orphanages. Child protection in the West is one thing: it is quite another here.' Hope sponsors two children in Romania and keeps in close touch with them.

But we must return to our chronology. After his time in Romania, Tuebrook and Orford, Hope moved on from parish ministry. This was not because he was dissatisfied but because, in the curiously discrete, unspoken way that these things happen within the Church of England, Hope's potential had been spotted. He was considered ready for his first senior appointment.

The Church was to stretch him, by testing him in an administrative role that required great political skill and fortitude: he was to take on what would undoubtedly be his most controversial appointment, becoming Principal of his old college, St Stephen's House, known as Staggers to its alumni.

In 1974, when Hope took over, St Stephen's was in crisis and facing possible closure. It was suffering from a culture of moral degeneracy and profound mismanagement. In a profile article on Hope, published in the *Sunday Telegraph* on 10 March 1991, an anonymous source is quoted as saying:

Frankly, the place was Sodom and Gomorrah. Rampant buggery everywhere and nearly everyone sodden with gin. They did a lovely choreography with plenty of incense and so on. I'm not saying it wasn't sincere or that they didn't have real faith; they did. But how could you take it all seriously in such an atmosphere of moral degeneracy?

There was some resentment of the measures Hope adopted to turn St Stephen's around. Some believed he had no empathy for the place and had not fitted in there when a student – was not a real 'Staggers-bag'. A source quoted in the *Sunday Telegraph* profile says of Hope the student: 'He was always going off to his room with migraines; he couldn't quite take the hot-house atmosphere. He kept to himself, got on with his doctoral thesis, and said his prayers.'

Hope certainly needed to say his prayers when he returned as Principal. He set out to bring Staggers into the twentieth century, and make it a key part of an attempt to give the Church of England a credible and alternative Catholicism which, in many ways, it was lacking. 'It was a big culture shock,' he says, 'going into that place straight from a parish.'

His Wakefield upbringing and loyalty to the Tractarian tradition within the Church were probably never more apparent than during his time here. One student who trained under him particularly remembers his early rising to say his daily prayers: 'No matter how early you got up, he was always in the chapel before you on his knees.' This led to something of a competition to see who could get there earlier. One ordinand finally thought he had won. At 5am the chapel was empty, but it turned out that the principal was away and, there-after, the competition was abandoned.

Hope forged a link, as he had been recommended to do, with the evangelical college Wycliffe Hall and shared teaching took place. Both institutions were under threat, and benefited from the savings. One of his great innovations, and one which is interesting in the context of his views on women's ordination, was to develop lay training courses for women – the first time any teaching had been offered to females in the history of the college. This is a pointer to the fact that Hope is not against women having a role in the Church – it is their taking a priestly or episcopal role that he cannot accept. His initiative was frowned upon by the *status quo*.

Some found his regime austere. The *Sunday Telegraph* profile has it that

David Hope introduced a draconian regime. Attendance at Morning and Evening Prayer was made compulsory on pain of dismissal. Students were forbidden to keep drink in their rooms.

Prospective students were told that all sexual activity unhallowed by the bonds of matrimony was forbidden, also on pain of dismissal. The liturgy was reformed, 'almost', said one student, 'out of existence'. The beautiful old vestments were disposed of and replaced by plain modern garments made of coarse materials.

Such interpretations do not do justice to Hope's aims, objectives and his great success in achieving them. Hope remembers his time at St Stephen's vividly:

> It was extremely difficult. I had to run the place, to do everything. I don't think I realized the extent of what needed to be done in terms of change, reform and trying to regain a reputation in Oxford and the wider Church. We had no married accommodation to speak of and we could not expand. So we were limited. Fortuitously, the Cowley Fathers had decided to leave their premises and they came to see me and said that they would be keen to move St Stephen's House from Norham Gardens to Cowley in east Oxford. Eventually it was decided to make the move and I had to oversee it.

The central importance of Hope's time as Principal cannot be underestimated – neither for St Stephen's as an institution nor in his later ministry. His time at Staggers was one of vision and growth. He learned how to come up with a plan for reform, and to carry it through in the teeth of opposition. He was showing himself as politically astute, determined, and resilient – qualities which would recommend him for even greater challenges. It wasn't simply that he had radically overhauled the regime, and cleaned the place up; he also developed a credible business plan, and oversaw investment in new buildings. In short, he turned Staggers around, and gave it a new lease of life. Hope had now shown himself to be a formidable administrator as well as a gifted priest, and marked himself out as a leader for the future.

As the 1980s dawned, and the English Church prepared to throw itself into a whirlpool of internal bickering and uncertainty over the ordination of women, Hope's track record identified him as a man who could well have a key role in preserving the unity of the Church. Among those who had noticed his potential was the future Archbishop of Canterbury, Robert Runcie, who later recalled: 'David is a very gifted and splendid bishop and lots of fun too. He did tremendous things at St Stephen's House and when he became Bishop of Wakefield I had no doubt that he would go on in the Church.'

Hope had spent over seven years in Oxford when a call came from Graham Leonard, then Bishop of London, with the suggestion that Hope become the next Vicar of All Saints, Margaret Street, in the heart of London's West End.

I had said that I would never work in London and the previous incumbent had just died of cancer. He had made it known that some members of the congregation had contributed to his ill-health. So not only did it look as if I was going to London, it was likely that I was on my way to a difficult situation. But this was the voice of the Lord calling me to another place that was in a mess – so I went to meet the churchwardens.

4

Home Again

Coming from the evangelical wing of the Church I have to say
that I was not terribly up to date with all the episcopal garb of
copes, mitres, chasubles and the likes and it was David who . . .
gave an extremely useful tutorial . . . as to what to wear, when to
wear it, how to proceed.

(George Carey)

David Hope's years as Vicar of All Saints, Margaret Street, were
enjoyable and fulfilling. All Saints, Hope's parish from 1982 to 1985,
is one of London's most beautiful and unique churches. Designed by
William Butterfield, it is a celebration of the Anglo-Catholic tradition
in its use of colour, light and space. Hope quickly made an impression
on his new parish, not least in reviving its music and liturgy.

The church is close to bustling Oxford Street and Soho. Hope had
a cosmopolitan congregation including both students and profession-
als. Within it was a strong gay element:

It was no more or less than quite a number of London churches
but, yes, it is fair to say there was a significant number of gay people
who worshipped there and I became friends with a good many of
them: musicians, entertainers, actors and so on – the kind of pro-
fessions which seem to have a high percentage of gay men and
women, and they were very much a part of the parish and community.

After the pressures of Oxford, Hope visibly relaxed and became more himself. His outrageous sense of humour and ability to respond to high camp were more in evidence. One story relates to his first Sunday at All Saints when a rather cocky young server whispered to his new incumbent that 'the priest doesn't sing hymns in the Sanctuary, Father'. Hope turned to the young upstart who was swinging his incense-laden thurible at great speed, glared at him and countered: 'I'll sing in my sanctuary if I want to; you get over there and swing your handbag.' Hope does not remember that tale but does recall the majesty of the worship in London's West End:

> You realize that you are just a very small part of a much greater mystery and it is through no deserving or ability of one's own. You are drawn by the grace of God into the heart of the mystery of the Eucharist, It is the whole event which draws you: the drama of the liturgy of which you are a part.
>
> Spiritually it was a very demanding parish. The church was open in my day from 6.30 in the morning until 8 at night and it was known as a place where anyone could drop in, very often anonymously, and unburden themselves, gain spiritual counsel, advice, or receive formal confession. The challenge was to try, in five minutes or so, to speak some word of hope, faith, comfort to someone you might never see again.

Despising the politics of some of the growing conflicts in the wider Church, Hope focused on parish life, celebrating the sacraments and preaching while, at the same time, enjoying the banter and social life which had thus far eluded him. He saw doubt and lack of authority in the decision-making process of the Church of England, and it worried him.

However, he could not entirely escape the great controversies of the day. One issue in the headlines concerned homosexuality. There were increasing moves to unmask people within the Church who were considered to be hiding their homosexual orientation. There were rumours about Hope's sexuality, about his relationships, and a desire to root out a partner, whether boyfriend or girlfriend. Because of this, Hope found it impossible to develop close friendships, or to have any visitor from out of town – straight or gay – staying over with him. At times, he found this intolerable – and it would get much worse when he became Bishop of London.

If we were to seek an explanation of why Hope is so private and withdrawn, much of the cause lies here. Under such scrutiny, Hope became more and more robust in the defence of his own time and space. He also became extremely confident on matters of theology. It is Hope's Catholicity which gives him a sense of belonging and destiny – which allows him to make decisions which affect the lives of other people. He is mild, and can be indecisive, in other ways – but not from a theological standpoint. His time as Vicar of All Saints, Margaret Street, further raised Hope's national profile. It was from here that he would, three years on in 1985, become a bishop in the Church of England.

Hope's standing in the Church is best understood by the fact that he would go straight from Vicar to Diocesan Bishop. This is very rare indeed. No suffragan bishop's job for him, nor a stint as archdeacon. Despite his clear relish of parish ministry, many believed that Hope's true vocation was to the episcopate. He was inspirational. This, allied with a gift for administration and management, made it seem to many in the Church hierarchy that a man with such gifts shouldn't be tele-scoping them into one fortunate parish when they could be illuminating a whole diocese.

Hope was chosen as Bishop of Wakefield in 1985. Ken Unwin was a member of the Crown Appointment's Commission which appointed him and, while recognizing the need for confidentiality even now, he agrees that there was a sense of excitement that the new Bishop was a local lad coming home.

We had clear criteria from the diocese as to the kind of bishop Wakefield needed after Colin James. Some suggested that Bishop Richard Hare should be promoted from his post as Suffragan Bishop of Pontefract. But there was also a desire for a younger man with fresh vision, and an acknowledgement that Wakefield might always be regarded as a good place for a new bishop to cut his teeth, to get to know the job. In the end the Commission recommended two names, of which David's was one.

There had been much speculation in the West Riding, none of which could go unnoticed by Hope's mother and sister. Anne Hope remembers: 'Mum and Dad were both really proud when David became Principal of St Stephen's House. I suppose they had been told that he was on the way to being a bishop.' Sadly, Jack died while David was at Margaret Street, but his mother lived to see his enthronement. Hope became, at 45, the youngest Diocesan Bishop in the Church of England.

As his name suggested, he offered hope not only to the Church of England but also to Anglo-Catholics, who feared what lay ahead on the question of women priests. He was regarded as talented, special: a parish priest at heart with obvious leadership skills. He was blunt, confident, genial . . . and probably full of fear. It was here that he had led those services for his family as a boy. He would be enthroned just feet from where he had sat as a choirboy.

His enthronement was an exciting and yet nerve-tingling experience. He was welcomed with an almost embarrassing fanfare of pomp and circumstance. He knew the diocese, and the diocese seemed to fall in love with him from the first moment. Succeeding the serious and reliable Colin James, who was translated (bishops are translated when they move from one diocese to another) south to the more senior post of Bishop of Winchester, Hope's new home was Bishop's Lodge – the large and rather grand residence of the Bishop of Wakefield which sits on the edge of the city.

But there is little that is grand about David Hope. He enjoys simple pleasures. One of his great joys in each of his episcopal jobs has been his weekly trip to the supermarket – Asda in Wakefield, Sainsbury's in London and Tesco in York. 'I suppose I do like shopping, but there's nothing strange about that. It's good to get the collar off and push a trolley around, particularly as I live on my own.' His hikes around Sainsbury's or Tesco help keep him sane. 'What a carry-on this morning with that Poll Tax march – I got caught up in it all, coming out of Sainsbury's' or, even more comically, one Saturday morning being engulfed in a Gay Pride march when various protesters were dressed as nuns and bishops. Hope was once spotted in the Tesco near Bishopthorpe Palace at 4.30am on Christmas Eve, having got out of bed to avoid that 'frightful rush'. A BBC camera crew was amused to see the new Archbishop of York carrying his episcopal robes around the Holy Land in a Tesco plastic carrier bag.

Hope made the move from London to Wakefield and settled into a small corner of one of the large living rooms at Bishop's Lodge. After the cramped flat 'above the shop' in Margaret Street he found the space and the vast garden rather embarrassing. The media made a lot of Hope's arrival back in White Rose country. BBC Radio Leeds broadcast his enthronement live. A series of people was interviewed before the service and all claimed to know David Hope the boy, David Hope the chorister, David Hope the local lad. 'It is amazing how many people suddenly have "I knew David Hope" stories' was one of the opening lines of his address from the pulpit of Wakefield Cathedral a few months after his consecration in York Minster.

Ken Unwin remembers the first senior staff meetings with David in the chair.

It is fair to say that David relied on us to teach him the ropes while being our pastor and Bishop. I mean, he had never been to a Diocesan Synod before and now he was President of one! There were issues about finance, appointments and property, and so on, which we were happy to explain to him. But, at the same time, his ability to get around the diocese, to meet people, to share his sense of mission and evangelism, was truly remarkable and we soon realized what it was about David Hope that was so special. It is also interesting that, while his suffragen Richard Hare could have adopted a more withdrawn kind of support for his younger boss, he didn't; in fact, the two men got on wonderfully well.

David's family was delighted to have him back in Yorkshire. David would take his Mum to rather grand functions and her life was to end on an upbeat note. Anne remembers: 'Mum was proud, and very nervous, soon after the consecration when David took her along as his 'partner' to Nostell Priory for a function with Lord and Lady St Oswald. But she need not have worried about getting it right. The hosts' daughter had a dog that was not housetrained and for the whole evening the dog kept peeing all over the floor to the point that my Mum didn't quite know what to say!'

Anne and David would gradually make up for their years apart, having ever more regular conversations on the telephone and growing closer together. Hope arrived back in Wakefield at a time of profound

change in the social fabric of Britain; change which threw up fundamental challenges for the Church. The year-long miners' strike was in
full swing, and Hope saw its effects within his diocese.

> Mrs Thatcher was, for many people, including myself, a figure of
> love and hate. I despised the way in which the miners were treated
> and heard the personal stories of misery and hopelessness which
> her government created in many of the mining communities in
> Yorkshire. She had no recognition whatsoever of what it meant to
> be down the pit, day after day, night after night. There was civil war
> between the Government and the communities. But I also recog-
> nized that the unions needed to be brought under greater control
> and that government had to govern. We needed a strong leader. I
> don't think the greater sense of people having more disposable
> income was really to do with Thatcherism – a greater sense of con-
> sumerism and choice was part and parcel of the day.

The great industries of the north – coal, textiles, steel and manu-
facturing – felt the full force of the new economic order of
competitiveness, the open market and much less trade union influence. Mines and mills closed because they were commercially
unviable. And, in all of this, the Church steadily began to lose its post-
war position within the community – witnessed perhaps most visibly
in the erosion of Sunday as the Sabbath. Shops were allowed to open
and pub hours extended. It was all a sign of the times.

Three other obvious undercurrents would also affect not only
Hope's time as Bishop of Wakefield but also his future ministry in
London and York. First, there was the rise of other faiths. Certain
parts of his new diocese, and much of the Diocese of London, contained British adherents to other faiths who wished to proclaim their
religious and cultural identity. While London was not bothered as a
city by any widespread discontent, areas such as Oldham and Bradford
showed early signs of general, community unrest – both from the
indigenous population, and from first- and second-generation immi-
grants from other cultures.

Hope was Bishop of Wakefield during the Salman Rushdie affair.
Rushdie's novel *The Satanic Verses* was regarded by some as an indirect
attack on Islam and its Prophet. The controversy provided a focus for

British Muslims who issued a *fatwa* against him. There were protests in many West Riding towns, and public libraries responded by removing the book from their shelves. It was a difficult time for Yorkshire Church of England schools, in many of which the majority of pupils are Muslim. Although much of the discontent was expressed in neighbouring Bradford, Hope had a lot to say on the need for understanding and co-operation in the cosmopolitan towns of Dewsbury, Batley, Wakefield, Halifax and Huddersfield, where there are large Muslim communities.

The second great change was in ecumenical relations. An awareness that, in a secular society, Christian churches from across the denominations would be more credible if they worked together, brought progress; sometimes painfully slowly. Hope played a full part in the West Yorkshire Ecumenical Council, which funded an ecumenical officer to work across denominational boundaries.

A generation emerged in the 1980s and 1990s which was simply unaware of Christian culture, and church attendances began to plummet. While the parish church was alive and well in many towns and villages in dioceses such as Wakefield, it was obvious that fewer and fewer residents were members and that the churches must find new ways forward. Hope faced this problem head-on as Bishop of Wakefield.

Third, women were achieving greater recognition in many areas, but not within the Church of England. The pressure on the Church to address this issue was overwhelming. Hope comprehended in depth the issues relating to women and the Church, knew how strong feelings were on both sides of the argument, and that it was crucial that the issue should not be allowed to split the Church.

> The key phrase in the Lambeth Resolution was how were we going to live together in the highest degree of communion. We were urged not to be too compromising but to respect the integrity of both sides. We were there to see if it was possible to devise some means of living together until the matter was resolved.

Hope admits that it was an impossible task:

If you wanted to go for pure Catholic theology it is impossible to believe that there was a way forward. But people were desirous of staying together in one communion, so inevitably there would be some imperfections and anomalies. To what degree can you live with anomalies until you sort these differences out? They will be sorted out one day but when? As with the great Christological disputes in the early life of the Church – these difficulties are eventually sorted out over time.

Presiding over this most difficult of times for the Church was Robert Runcie, who was consecrated Archbishop of Canterbury in 1980. His style was relaxed, liberal, academic. There was tremendous energy focused on inner-city ministry. Runcie was essentially a conciliator when it came to the pressing questions of the Church. He was a liberal Anglo-Catholic, although the Anglo-Catholic community felt betrayed by his refusal to confront the ongoing liberalization of church doctrine and practice.

The resentment came to a head with the anonymous denunciation in *Crockford's Clerical Directory* in 1987, which accused Runcie of being an 'elitist liberal, taking the line of least resistance on each issue'. The author proved to be a former friend and Oxford academic, Dr Garry Bennett, who later committed suicide over the furore that his article caused. Runcie's archiepiscopate will be remembered for the many controversial situations he found himself in. He had numerous clashes with the Conservative government and his former university friend, Mrs Thatcher. Through the Church's Commission on Urban Priority Areas he supported the Church's right to speak out on social and economic issues. The report *Faith in the City* was one of the most significant Church of England documents of the twentieth century, foolishly lambasted by the government when it first appeared. The report argued that economic policies should be judged 'morally' and recommended a massive increase in public expenditure to alleviate poverty in the inner cities. This was not an idea that appealed to Margaret Thatcher.

She was also irritated by Runcie's even-handed sermon at the service of thanksgiving for victory in the Falklands War in July 1982. In his sermon he stressed that Britain should look to reconciliation rather than triumphalism in victory, and while this might have been morally acceptable, politically it was not good PR.

Runcie always adopted the policy of 'Don't ask' when it came to those he ordained whom he suspected might be gay. This, perhaps rightly, infuriated many conservatives within the Church, who suggested that he was being naïve and even dishonest. Reluctantly, Runcie accepted that he must take part in the General Synod vote on future legislation for women priests. The Church was deeply divided on the issue and both sides were frustrated by the Archbishop's refusal to reveal, once again, his own opinion.

Hope disapproved strongly of this drift, and lack of firm leadership. He was not in a position to alter it, but in Wakefield he could get on with things. He cut a dashing figure. Handsome, energetic, confident, Bishop David went about his diocese saying hello, popping in for coffee, occasionally being outrageous and relishing his local connections: 'Hello Frank, how's your mother . . . Oh I didn't know, I am sorry.' Impeccably turned out, simple, and economical in every sense of the word, the new Bishop made friends quickly.

He appointed Tim Thornton, a former student from St Stephen's House, as his chaplain – an appointment which turned out to be one of the most important he would make as a bishop. Relationships between bishops and their chaplains are either notoriously good or bad but rarely indifferent. Tim, now Bishop of Sherborne, admired Hope and endeavoured not only to support him but also to protect him from others – and himself – when appropriate.

Tim was popular with most clergy and certainly with the vast majority of those who visited Bishop's Lodge. He would greet people with genuine warmth and pave the way for that important interview, encounter, or argument with the new Bishop: 'You'll have to watch him today: he got in late last night and he's out again in an hour but he really wanted to see you.' Such accurate intelligence was invaluable for a young priest facing an audience with his bishop.

Later, in York, Mike Kavanagh would serve Hope for almost a decade as his trusted chaplain. 'My key memories of Bishop David will be sitting silently together in chapel before Mass, and a sense of peaceful togetherness. It feels like the wellspring from which other things flow. There is a feeling of being caught up in a bigger story.'

It was during this time that I met Hope for the first time. As presenter of the BBC Radio Leeds Sunday breakfast show and the Bishop of Bradford's Diocesan Communications Officer, I developed an easy relationship with Hope. We had a similar sense of humour and the Bishop would occasionally summon me for a pub lunch to talk about church matters. I used to write for the *Church of England Newspaper* and later the *Church Times* as their northern reporter and this gave me additional reasons to seek out Hope's views and opinions. His Communications Officer, Roy Clements, now a priest in Mirfield and a Canon of Wakefield Cathedral, respected this wider relationship and used to laugh knowingly if Hope had told me something 'in confidence' for future use. It was never a problem.

Hope took a great interest in those agencies which would be in contact with his flock when they were in need: the hospice movement, the marriage guidance counselling service Relate. He was concerned about housing, education and homelessness. His success as Bishop of Wakefield is well gauged by the love and affection that ordinary parishioners still have for him and by the sheer number of people who travelled down to London to his enthronement as Bishop of London. But the centenary celebrations of the formation of the Wakefield Diocese, in 1988, were the greatest success for Hope. Filling the Huddersfield Town football stadium with tens of thousands of worshippers, establishing a mission fund of £1 million and leaving behind a culture and understanding of the true purposes of the Church for mission were concrete reminders of Hope's time in the West Riding.

A future *Sunday Telegraph* portrait of Hope would emphasize his pastoral gifts: 'He has been, by all accounts, a great success in Wakefield. He is good with people, unlike some bishops who feel they ought to have a common touch, he is good at being friendly without embarrassing matiness. He smiles from his eyes; his manner appears completely devoid of artificiality.' The strength of the *Sunday Telegraph* piece is its recognition that he would one day become Archbishop of York: 'It is true that he would like in the end to go to York, there are many fellow Yorkshiremen who hope his ambition will be fulfilled.'

Hope's sense of ministry relied heavily on the Tractarian view nurtured in his childhood in the cathedral in which he now sat as Bishop. He has a high view of the sacraments, takes preparation for preaching extremely seriously, but is at heart a pastor. Here is the heart of ministry: a priest with his people at significant times (birth, marriage, death) but also in those humdrum moments – calling the bingo numbers, washing up, having a drink.

In some ways the Church took Hope away from what he was best at when it made him Bishop. His skills as a pastor, as one of the people, were neutralized by the organizational structure of the Church, which imposed numerous committees, meetings and groups – often in London – on his time. Then there were the three Synod meetings a year (two in London, one in York) to add to the work load.

As Hope was increasingly pulled away from ministry he came to question what he was about, but this also made him extraordinarily considerate and supportive of the parish clergy – as long as they were committed, had drive and an enthusiasm for the Gospel. He admired hard-working parish priests. Perhaps he was slightly jealous of them. He was quick to praise endeavour in parish life, regular and committed prayer rooted in a local community, well-organized churches and parishes, centres of worship and outreach which had a verve and missionary strategy, and he regularly made the effort to pen a note of encouragement and congratulation.

It was while Hope was still Bishop of Wakefield, but when rumour was rife that he was bound for London, that he met Christopher Morgan. Morgan was then a reporter for the BBC's *Sunday* programme but would later become religious affairs correspondent of the *Sunday Times*. Morgan was instantly struck by the unique qualities which he saw in the young Bishop. He remembers: 'I invited him to have lunch with me at L'Amico's restaurant – a discreet eating place in Westminster. It was the day Hope was to receive his pass as the newest member of the House of Lords as Bishop of Wakefield. During the lunch I said to him emphatically that he would move from Wakefield to London and then on to be Archbishop of York. David laughed at this. In fact he told me that if it came true he would take me out to lunch at the Dorchester. He never has, by the way!'

Morgan remembers, a few weeks after that, doing a piece on the *Sunday* programme where he confidently predicted Hope's translation to London. The following day he received a telephone call from Thornton, Hope's chaplain, asking what he was up to and stressing how happy they were with things in the Diocese of Wakefield.

It was also about this time that Hope met the future Archbishop of Canterbury, George Carey. Hope was already a Bishop while Carey was still Principal of Trinity Theological College. It was in this capacity that Carey had been asked to chair a commission, in 1987, to look into the Garry Bennett Crockford's 'Preface' controversy. Carey was to report his commission's findings to the House of Bishops, and it was Hope who would present the commission's report. Carey remembers Hope's pastoral touch:

We knew of each other – we had both been principals of theological colleges, even though they were from rather different traditions – but we didn't really get to know one another until David helped me in presenting the findings of that commission to the House of Bishops.

One of the first times I can actually say that David and I became real friends, rather than acquaintances, was when I was appointed Bishop of Bath and Wells. Coming from the evangelical wing of the Church I have to say that I was not terribly up to date with all the episcopal garb of copes, mitres, chasubles and the likes and it was David who, quietly and so helpfully, gave an extremely useful tutorial as Bishop of Wakefield to the new Bishop of Bath and Wells as to what to wear, when to wear it, how to proceed.

Within two years Carey had succeeded Robert Runcie, and Hope was Bishop of London. The two of them lived just a short distance from each other across Lambeth Bridge for nearly five years. The relationship was not without its tense moments, particularly over the ordination of women. But once Hope had succeeded John Habgood at York, things improved and the two enjoyed what Carey characterizes as 'a solid working relationship and friendship. David is warm, open, in many ways a typical Yorkshireman. He is kind, never cruel, blunt.' Carey would increasingly rely on Hope as his archiepiscopal ministry approached its finale.

Wakefield had to give in to the inevitable when Hope was announced as the 131st Bishop of London on 18 February 1991. After six years, and now aged 50, Hope would become third in seniority within the Church of England hierarchy after Canterbury and York. It was John Major's first episcopal appointment as Prime Minister. Hope had received a letter on a Friday morning inviting him to go to the capital. He opened the envelope, marked PRIVATE AND CONFIDENTIAL, and read the contents. The following Sunday evening, he rang me shortly after I had returned home after taking Evensong at St Mary the Virgin, Embsay, near Skipton: 'Rob, I have had a word with Bishop Roy [my boss] – he says it is OK for us to meet – and I would very much like you to come over and see me tomorrow because there is something I would like to discuss with you.'

When I arrived at Bishop's Lodge for a sandwich lunch, he produced the letter. He looked slightly agitated and, in retrospect, was probably furious. It was a great opportunity, but he was happy in Yorkshire. Issues such as women priests and homosexuality coupled with a realization that an evangelical, George Carey, would be leading from the front across the river at Lambeth Palace made the whole prospect less than attractive. We discussed the kind of questions he might be asked at his first press conference in London and I prepared some suggestions in the first briefing I was ever asked to do for David Hope. It would be the first of many.

Hope's own message to his Wakefield congregations was characteristically modest:

> The announcement of my appointment to the See of London will come, I suspect, as much as a surprise to you, as the arrival of the letter from the Prime Minister was to me. I was obviously aware that my name had been rumoured, among others. I had begun to hope that the invitation had gone elsewhere and been accepted; in the event it had not. It was the most difficult and agonizing decision I've had to make in my life. Now it is made, I do ask you to keep me in your prayers, and to pray for those who have the responsibility of appointing the new Bishop of Wakefield.

Reaction to the appointment in the media was predictable. Emphasis was placed on the fact that he was a bachelor and that he was going back to London where he had been a priest before moving to Wakefield. Damian Thompson, then religious affairs correspondent for the *Daily Telegraph*, emphasized that Hope was 'determined to heal the rift' between opponents and proponents of women priests while Revd Jeremy Haselock, then Chaplain to the Bishop of

Chichester, issued the following statement: 'He's an excellent liturgist and a splendid administrator and very good at presiding over public worship. He's also got a mischievous streak in him which will be a very healthy influence in the world of London Anglo-Catholicism.'

Nerissa Jones, a campaigner for women's ministry, who was then Curate at St Botolph's, Aldgate, was also optimistic: 'Things have not been easy for women in London. If Dr Hope is being gentle in his approach, that is really good. It won't frighten the other side either.'

One of the most upbeat and optimistic assessments of the potential for good came from the then *Times* columnist Clifford Longley:

Hope has already indicated that he will accept the ordination of women if it happens, trying to hold the Church together. If he can persuade his fellow Anglo-Catholics to do the same he will at least have delivered them from their present condition of siege. He would do even better to revive the agenda of Anglo-Catholic renewal which was starting to take shape before the ordination of women issue knocked it off course. That means persuading them that they still have something to offer the rest of the Church. And, ultimately, that means persuading them to love the Church of England again – as it is, not as they dream of it.

Hope was focusing on the task ahead in London. In an interview with the new Archbishop of Canterbury's son Andrew Carey, who works for the *Church of England Newspaper*, the new Bishop of London gave some intriguing insights into the themes that would take up a good deal of his episcopate. He spoke at length of waiting to listen to the arguments before deciding which way to vote on women priests (a carefully worded statement on such a thorny issue) reminding his interviewer that the Church of England is part of the One Holy Catholic and Apostolic Church whether it likes it or not.

'I believe that the Spirit guides the Church,' said Hope, 'but we must be open to the prompting of the Spirit.' At the time of the interview the first, inconclusive Gulf War was raging: 'I am troubled and sickened by the Gulf War. I have to say that resort to war is always a failure. I wish there were some other way to resolve this conflict. But in the real world I believe that we are involved in a war that is just.'

And all of this while still at home in lovely Yorkshire. But not for long. The furniture van was booked. St Paul's Cathedral was gearing up for a wondrous enthronement. The capital challenge was about to begin.

5

Bed of Nails

Everybody who met him emerged with greater affection and respect for the Bishop and greater warmth and responsiveness towards the wider Church. He made it all seem easy but it certainly was not and takes a closer observer to realize the magnitude of the achievement.

(Richard Chartres, Bishop of London)

Richard Chartres, David Hope's successor as Bishop of London, is generous in his summary of Hope's time there. Hope and Chartres are totally different characters yet, despite a few prickly moments on certain issues, there is a genuine warmth and respect between them. Chartres says: 'The effect of David Hope's ministry on the Diocese of London was dramatic. We were in the doldrums when he was appointed and much distracted by the debate on the ordination of women. Diocesan leadership had been preoccupied with many extra-diocesan agendas.' Impressed with the sheer vigour and energy with which Hope applied himself to the job, Chartres points to the heavy workload: 'David's determination to focus on the diocese and a punishing schedule of visits to parishes and schools transformed the atmosphere in a very short time and restored some credibility to the episcopate.'

Chartres, who was promoted by Hope to join the senior staff team as Bishop of Stepney (after the late and much-loved Jim Thomson was translated to Bath and Wells) recalls how Hope worked at team building: 'He had a hard job building a greater sense of collegiality between members of a rather divided diocesan team but the Agenda for Action process [more about that later] was particularly important in giving us all a common focus which built unity.'

But it was Hope's personality and approach which held the key for Chartres: 'After every single one of David's visits there was apprecia-tion of his down-to-earth good humour and his support and encouragement for church life.'

Everyone had a view on the state of the Diocese of London as the new Bishop prepared for his enthronement. Most agreed that Hope had a gargantuan task ahead of him. He would certainly make enemies, as well as friends. There was concern at the deep divisions on women priests and over the Church's attitude to homosexuality.

The morning of David Hope's enthronement, on the Feast of the Holy Cross, 14 September, was a beautiful one. There was hope and optimism in the air. The Bishop must have been full of trepidation, but he certainly did not show it. He was strengthened and encouraged by the conviction that God's will was being done. He had said many times that he would not be the next Bishop of London, but had now bowed to the inevitable.

A specially chartered train from Wakefield was en route to King's Cross. The 'Hope Express' was packed with friends and former parishioners from the deaneries and parishes. St Paul's Cathedral was filled to capacity. The wider Church of England waited for Hope's arrival with anticipation – as the third most senior figure in the Church of England, he would have to balance the churchmanship between Lambeth Palace and Bishopthorpe.

George Carey was making a heavy start as Archbishop of Canter-bury, attracting a series of negative headlines. In an interview with *Reader's Digest*, the question of the integrity of those opposed to the ordination of women arose and Carey said it was 'a heresy' to say that women could not be ordained. This led not only to outrage among opponents, but also to the suggestion more widely in the Church that he lacked political nous and was not up to the job. John Habgood, Archbishop of York and the most experienced and erudite leader of the Anglican Church in Britain, had assumed the role of elder states-man, but neither he nor Carey fully appreciated the Catholic psyche and the level of insecurity and resentment which was building. The Diocese of London had become a ghetto containing individuals with polarized views and interests. Under Hope's predecessor, Bishop

Leonard, the Diocese had been detached, aloof. The bishop's office, his 'inner cabinet' and his secretariat had been handpicked and were extremely loyal, which enforced a bunker mentality. For David Hope the expectations of his ministry and arrival were intense and concentrated. Something had to be done to dissipate the poisonous atmosphere and improve ministry within the diocese.

The Church of England was facing an enormous task in the capital. The Diocese of London covers a vast span north of the River Thames with the Diocese of Southwark taking care of the area to the south. It was soon to be announced that Hope's neighbour from Wakefield, the Bishop of Bradford, Roy Williamson, was moving south to be Southwark's next bishop. With 3.2 million people, the largest population of any Anglican diocese in the communion, London has 25 deaneries and over 450 parishes, but fewer than 50,000 people go to church regularly. Many Victorian church buildings must be maintained on tight budgets. Parishes generally have small electoral rolls. Several, where there is a concentration of hotels and offices, have almost no residents. Many rely on commuters who give London that eclectic feel: a real mish-mash of people from a wide variety of places.

The diocesan offices are located near the Tate Gallery in Pimlico, just across the road from the headquarters of MI5. Archdeacon Derek Hayward was Diocesan Secretary when Hope arrived, and ran the office in a genial, old-fashioned way. His meetings would be conducted in his large room with refreshments laid on – a substantial spread of sandwiches, fruit and drinks. There were many clergymen on his staff who had moved from parish ministry into administrative jobs. While happy and family-oriented, there was a distinct lack of verve and professionalism. It was not business-like – and it certainly was not Church House, Wakefield!

Apart from the Westminster home of the diocesan bishop and the Causton Street diocesan office, St Paul's Cathedral was the other main centre of diocesan activity and ministry, run in Hope's time under the former Dean, the Very Revd Eric Evans. Unfortunately, while St Paul's was doing an excellent job fulfilling its international and national roles, it sometimes fell down on its diocesan responsibilities, and the far-flung parishes did not feel as if St Paul's was their Mother Church. The deaneries are divided into five episcopal areas: London, Stepney, Willesden, Kensington and Edmonton, each (apart from

London) with their own area bishop. These, plus St Paul's Cathedral and the diocesan office and a wide range of boards, officers and committees, provided Hope with significant ecclesiological and practical problems.

From the borders of Heathrow Airport, sweeping east towards Essex, the London Diocese spans a great diversity of cultures and peoples. But it is also home to many – the homeless, the addicted and the vulnerable – who find life tough, demanding, even impossible. There are also hundreds of thousands of tourists. It is a potent mix. Although the diocese raised around £12 million every year during Hope's time, most of the cash was spent on buildings rather than people – something Hayward, as General Secretary, was keen to change. Hope was particularly vexed about the future of the 36 churches in the Square Mile, some of the most architecturally stunning in the capital.

'London is a fascinating and extremely beautiful city, once you find your way around it; as a diocese it raises big questions about pastoral oversight and care,' said Hope on the eve of his enthronement. The *Church Times* described Hope's challenge as 'a bed of nails' on which he would have to lie. Hope kept his own counsel on most things. During five years in London he almost never mentioned the name of his predecessor, Graham Leonard. The difficulty was (and this came as a great disappointment to disciples of Leonard) that, although Hope concurred with many of the opinions he expressed, there was absolutely no point in making a fresh start as Bishop and then following the same battle plan.

Walter Schwarz, then religious affairs correspondent of the *Guardian*, made these pertinent comments six months after Hope's enthronement: 'Nobody knows the number of bishops who would revolt against Canterbury and York. Graham Leonard, former leader of the opposition to women priests, has retired as Bishop of London and his successor, though against women priests, has declined to take up the mantle.'

Hope had his own agenda to follow, his own priorities. So, despite the huge odds against him, contrary to the advice of many, and in the face of the general cynicism of staunch Catholics, Hope endeavoured to put mission back at the top of the agenda in the capital.

Hope puts a positive spin on the situation he found himself in:

> I was aware of the massive resources – of people, buildings, finance, expertise – across a wide range of different disciplines and specialities. But the diocese did not seem to have any priorities – to know where it was going and why – and though the coal face of the Church is obviously at parish level and the diocese should not interfere in that, there should be guidelines, points of emphasis, a working together along broad lines for the sake of the Gospel.

This was classic Hope. The obvious potential conflict between imposing a mission strategy from the centre and perpetuating a sense of drift and a lack of coherence had to be avoided.

As the enthronement procession made its way under Wren's vast and splendid dome, with Hope resplendent in his new gold and white London cope and mitre, with many of London's most famous churches embroidered over it, the task facing him was truly exceptional. Would he rise to it? What would be his hallmark? I was enormously privileged to be the only member of the congregation in Hope's private chapel earlier that morning. As Hope recalled: 'I celebrated the Eucharist at home, a very appropriate way of preparing for the quite remarkable events later, but I honestly did not become consumed by all the fuss and excitement.' As well as representatives from the Dioceses of Wakefield and London, also present were the religious communities, livery companies, ecumenical and interfaith representatives, the joint choirs of Wakefield and St Paul's Cathedral, along with the Lord Mayor of London. You could discern the sense of joy, relief and optimism in the congregation as Hope was enthroned. Here was a relatively young man with a sense of mission and service for the Gospel.

From that morning Hope became a member of the Privy Council and was entitled to take his seat in the House of Lords for the second time. Hope picked 'To the Name that Brings Salvation', 'In the Cross of Christ I Glory', 'Ye Watchers and Ye Holy Ones' and 'Crown Him with Many Crowns' as hymns for the service. The music was an impressive mix of liturgical celebration.

Mr Dean, I, David, by Divine permission Lord Bishop of London, thank you for your welcome into this cathedral church. I ask the prayers of all my people that I may be to them a faithful pastor and true Father in God, that we may serve together our London to the honour and glory of Christ; and desire that I may be inducted, installed and enthroned as Bishop of the Diocese of London, according to the mandate of the Most Reverend Father in God, George, By Divine Providence Lord Archbishop of Canterbury.

But it was the word 'courtesy' which dominated his first statements as ✠David Londin. It was the word Hope wanted people to remember from his enthronement sermon – and one he would come back to time and again during his years as Bishop of London. He was influenced by the words of Mother Julian of Norwich whose phrase 'Our good and courteous Lord' he saw as a watchword for society and all its divisions. Hope appealed to the diocese, gathered in that solemn and symbolic moment of welcome and enthronement, to extend a common courtesy to one another. He said differences across a range of issues 'should not be occasions for strife'. Churchgoers should rejoice in the rich diversity God gave rather than write off people of different opinions. 'Only so shall we be preserved from declining into a cosy congregationalism, a suffocating parochialism, a ghettoism which has never been an aspect of proper understanding of the Church of which we are called to be a part.' The chief characteristic of this courtesy would be listening. Instead of taking entrenched positions on this issue or that, people should listen to one another by extending a common courtesy.

Already, Hope had upped the stakes. Mother Julian's message had been updated and was strongly rooted in a twentieth-century context. His address coincided with a hard-hitting speech by the then Conservative Agriculture Minister John Gummer about the future of the Church. Gummer's warning was gloomy: 'We are very close to disintegration. Unless we call a halt now, orthodox believers will be driven out and the Church of England will become a sect.' Several politicians who were deeply disenchanted with the Church of England used a political platform to push their theological views. Hope disapproved, questioning what authority they had for doing so.

Because so many of the seats in St Paul's Cathedral were taken up by specially invited guests and people from Wakefield, Bishop Hope had asked for a Eucharist on the Sunday evening, also in St Paul's, which would be open to all. Hope intended that these two services should be related. His sermon in the evening was equally crafted and was, in a way, more important to him. This was more of a family, diocesan occasion, and something which had been rarely held. Hope used many themes which he would later develop as Bishop of London and Archbishop of York. He reminded his new troops that Sunday is a special day – the first day of the week, a Christian day of celebration. He quoted Michael Ramsey: 'It is joy experienced by those who, come what may, are beginning to know God, to enjoy God in his beauty and loveliness and to be exposed to his energies.' And then he pleaded once again for a Gospel-based Church which is more at ease with itself: 'So we need to keep the lines open, the lines of friendship and hospitality, of exchange, of prayer and worship and sacramental life together, especially and particularly with those with whom we disagree.'

Rejoicing, reconciliation and renewal were to be central themes from the very beginning of Hope's tenure. They were certainly not easily achievable. Media interest in Hope was, by now, intense. *Heart of the Matter* – the BBC TV Sunday evening documentary – was already putting together a fly-on-the-wall film on Hope (to be called *One Church, One Faith, One Sex*) and he developed a friendship with the team during the three-month project: 'Not you lot again! Oh dear' Hope would say when he realized that the cameras were at yet another event. During the first weeks of his ministry, Hope was filmed at the Remembrance Day Service at the Cenotaph, the General Synod, a confirmation at St Botolph's, Aldgate and a specially arranged climb to the top of the dome of St Paul's Cathedral. He was also filmed at Oak Hill Theological College, on a visit to the Harrow Deanery, and at the consecration of his two new bishops (Richard Chartres and Graham Dow – eventually Bishops of London and Carlisle respectively) at St Paul's Cathedral.

Hope does not like writing. He finds it time-consuming and feels he has little to say that is worthy of committing to paper. So Morag Reeve, then of Darton, Longman & Todd, came up with what for him was an attractive proposal; that they should publish many of the addresses and speeches from his first year as Bishop of London. In a letter to him, Ms Reeve explained: 'What we have in mind is a book that takes the best of your sermons, talks and articles in your first year or so as Bishop, and presents a coherent picture of your thinking on certain key issues of faith. I think it would be important for it to be put together with a clear sense of unity about themes and issues.' Hope somewhat reluctantly agreed and the book – *Living the Gospel* – was published in 1993. This was only his second book following *Friendship with God* in 1985. The only other book he wrote during his time as Bishop was *Signs of Hope*, a collection of sermons and addresses drawn from his first five years as Archbishop of York, and published by Continuum in 2000.

One of his first public engagements after his enthronement was an evening at the home of the then editor of the *Church Times*, John Whale, and his wife Judy. Hope walked into the house in St James' Walk, EC1 on a damp November evening to find a cluster of staff including the late and much-missed Betty Saunders, Glynn Paflin (now news editor) and Rupert Shortt. Also present were Whale's secretary, Yolande Clarke and Roy Reynoldson, a former printer. For decades, relationships between the *Church Times* and the Bishop of London had been formal, to say the least, and Whale was keen to establish a more relaxed and rigorous rapport between the Church's main weekly and the new Bishop. Betty Saunders had enjoyed writing as Sidesman in the diary of the *Church Times* just after the enthronement when she explained how Hope was managing in the cramped conditions of London House. She brings Hope's views on the house to life:

> He likes the kitchen: white and bright (not new, he says, but the Church Commissioners have done it up very nicely) and he has made the former dining room his sitting room. It has a smaller, homelier look than the (slightly) larger room which will accommodate his dinner guests.

Saunders mentioned the Yorkshire mementos from his previous home and the view of Westminster Abbey 'which delighted him'.

One of the early themes which Hope latched on to was the Chief Rabbi's suggestion that what was needed was not so much a Decade of Evangelism (recently launched) but 'a Decade of Renewal'. The

1. David Hope, aged approximately seven years,
with his sister Anne.

(Anne Hope)

2. January 1949.
(Anne Hope)

3. David Hope (far right), in his uniform for the
Queen Elizabeth Grammar School, at home with his family.
(Anne Hope)

4. David Hope coming out of Liverpool Cathedral after his ordination in June 1966. Pictured with his mother (to his right) and Auntie Phyllis.

(Anne Hope)

5. Hope, as Bishop of Wakefield, dressed for the first time in convocation robes. (1985)

(Wakefield Diocesan Library)

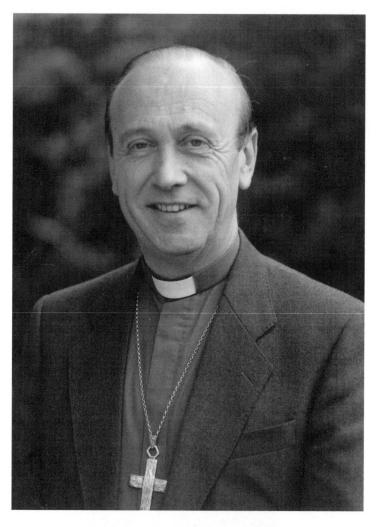

6. Portrait of Hope prior to his enthronement as Bishop of London, 1991.

7. Dr David Hope with David Bellamy at the launch for 'Yews for the Millennium'. An ancient yew tree was offered to every parish in Britain to mark the millennium of Jesus' birthday. (1999)

8. Hope visiting Selby coalfields before their closure in 2001.
(Bishopthorpe Palace Picture Library)

9. Hope with North Yorkshire schoolchildren.
(Evening Press York)

10. Mount of Olives, Jerusalem. Hope talking to director Patrick Hargreaves during the filming of a BBC documentary on the eve of his enthronement as Archbishop of York.

Bishop felt that the Rabbi had hit the nail on the head. There was so much latent religion and faith in people: what was needed was to bring that faith out. Hope was invited to give a lunchtime lecture in early October at The Nave in Uxbridge and it was on this occasion that he first met the then Rector of Uxbridge, Michael Colclough, and his wife Cynthia. Michael would later work very closely with David Hope at London House and the two men hit it off straight away. Hope told his audience: 'I like the phrase "Decade of Renewal" because there is a great deal for us in our Church to renew.'

By now Hope was in third gear. He was enjoying the immense challenge and was generally warmly welcomed. Of course there were some who were cynical, dubious and unkind. They suspected he would 'do a Leonard' when push came to shove on the vexed issue of women in the priesthood, and vote against. But Hope took every opportunity to talk about London, the Church and mission. The new Bishop felt, in doing so, the Church connected well with 'the average person in the pew'. No one could accuse Bishop Hope of keeping a low profile in those early months. He set about his task with a vengeance and quickly made an impression both as a pastoral Bishop, which London had not really had under Leonard, and as a manager looking at the future of ministry and mission.

An example of the kind of event Hope enjoyed because it mixed these two – ministry and mission – together well was the 25th anniversary service of Shelter – which campaigns on behalf of the homeless – at St Martin in the Fields. This was a big occasion with national news coverage; a large congregation with the great and the not so great and Prunella Scales, the actress, reading a lesson. She said: 'The plight of the homeless is a concern for us all. This service will provide a means for us to focus our concerns and to offer our prayers and thanksgiving for all that Shelter does to help those who have no home.'

Despite his Anglo-Catholic background, Hope was aware of the expectations of the evangelicals and charismatics. Many of them were suspicious. These were the early days of Holy Trinity Brompton's amazing growth and the advent of the Alpha Course – a nation-wide teaching programme adopted by many churches. There were key centres of growth in Brompton, Marylebone and Northwood. Hope gave these parishes his support and welcomed the good news of growth. In his first presidential address to the Diocesan Synod on 29 October, just six weeks after his enthronement, he called for an imaginative and positive strategy for mission within the diocese as a whole. He told elected clergy and lay members of the Synod that London posed a particular challenge. It was the responsibility of the diocese in the Decade of Evangelism to take seriously its response to the resolution at the Lambeth Conference in 1988. This called for 'a shift to dynamic missionary emphasis going beyond care and nurture to proclamation and service . . . Not only am I committed to making a statement about the need for a mission strategy in the diocese, I am equally committed to putting it into practice.'

6

Schism

It was tough, I can tell you. But I really did everything I could to make things work not only for the Diocese of Southwark but also for David Hope across the river. It was strange, eventually taking that first ordination service in St Paul's Cathedral of all those women now to be priested, and all I can say is that I did it to ensure that we stayed together in our differences.

(Bishop Roy Williamson)

Some parishes had not seen a Bishop of London for years. Hope began a series of deanery visits aimed at introducing him across the diocese. A deanery is a grouping of parishes under an area (or rural) dean. But it was not just to the churches that Hope went. He wanted to meet the whole community, the Church in the world. This made an immediate impression on many of those outside the Church who came into contact with him.

The cynics were alarmed about the intentions of the new Bishop. He clearly intended to get to know the diocese and for the diocese to know him. To understand how demanding these 25 individual deanery days were, one itinerary gives an example of what was involved. On 2 October 1991, he spent the day with the clergy and people of the Brent Deanery in north London, where several people had worked hard to produce an exciting and varied programme. He left London House early, driven by his chauffeur, Fred, and accompanied by his chaplain, Tim Thornton, arriving in the deanery by 9am. He said Morning Prayer with the clergy and ministers of the Church on the Rise covenanting group (Anglicans, Roman Catholics,

Methodists and United Reformed) before going into a local home for coffee and biscuits. Many people were bemused that the Bishop of London was actually here, with them, for the day. During a short meeting over coffee he heard of the problems faced by refugees in that part of Brent. Asylum was an increasingly difficult issue in the deanery where a Vicar, Peter Stubbs, showed Hope around a new church complex: flats for 21 people and a worship centre as well as various rooms and a church hall for use by the community. John Gill, a churchwarden, was also present. At 10.30am, he was at the office of Brent Welcare, meeting representatives including the chairwoman, Griselda Tyler. He was particularly impressed with the Anglican involvement in local community work and wanted to learn more about the work of the diocese with refugees and their families. Then there were more visits: to churches, shopping centres and a school, followed by a service for the whole deanery, after which Hope returned to Westminster, exhausted but exhilarated. He was meeting people. He was being seen, being heard and, above all, listening to the needs of London.

His first overseas visit as ✠David Londin was a trip to Istanbul for the enthronement of Bartholomew I as Archbishop of Constantinople. He enjoyed this Orthodox experience immensely: 'There is something wonderfully cut and thrust about the Orthodox way of doing things,' said Hope, remembering his time in Bucharest. 'It could have been 398 and the occasion of the enthronement of John Chrysostom. But instead, it was Saturday 2 November 1991 and the occasion of the new Oecumenical Patriarch and Archbishop of Constantinople. The small Anglican delegation was part of a crowd packed like sardines into the tiny Church of the Phanar which now serves as the Patriarchal Cathedral.'

There was much pushing and shoving, and once in the church there was no way anyone could get out! The ceremony itself was simple and adorned only with the handing over of the staff, a blessing on the new patriarch, and his ascending of the Patriarchal Throne – a 'throne' which it is claimed goes back to the time of John Chrysostom. It was clear to all present that we were participating in yet another phase of history in the Church Universal and the Church down the ages.

Hope relished being part of this great tradition:

> Patriarchs from Alexandria and Antioch as well as Romania and
> Bulgaria; the Archbishops of Thyateria and Caesarea among others
> were there, together with many clergy, monks, nuns and lay people
> – all greeted by the new Patriarch. Cardinal Cassidy led a high del-
> egation from the Vatican, which was significant in the light of the
> recently reported remarks of the Patriarch of Russia and others
> about, as they see it, the Roman Church's imperialism in tradition-
> ally Orthodox lands.
>
> Our small delegation consisted of myself on behalf of the Arch-
> bishop of Canterbury, Dr John Fenwick from Lambeth Palace,
> Bishop Mark Dwyer of Bethlehem, United States of America who
> is co-Chair of the Anglican Orthodox Joint Doctrinal Dialogue,
> [and] the Archdeacon Geoffrey Evans, on behalf of the Bishop of
> Gibraltar in Europe. [We were] acknowledged warmly by the
> Patriarch in his formal address as he spoke of our close relationship
> over the years.

Hope loved the ceremony of it all:

> The shouts of axios were loud and prolonged at various points in
> the two-and-a-half hour ceremony. They seemed strangely incon-
> gruous, however, in the contemporary setting of the ballroom of a
> modern hotel set out for the vast reception and luncheon which
> unfortunately we had to leave [for the airport] after the first of what
> was promised to be quite a number of courses.
>
> There were many promises of prayerful support, many expres-
> sions of goodwill and hope for the future. But Patriarch
> Bartholomew will need calm nerves and a cool head as he seeks to
> secure his own Church's survival in a place where already it finds
> itself severely circumscribed.

As the build-up to the set-piece General Synod debate on the ordination of women continued, Church of England dioceses were asked
to debate the issue across the country and vote. London was the last
diocese of the 44 to vote on the draft. Hope was aware that the
national media would focus on London not only because it was the

last but because of the colourful characters on just about every side of the debate (and there were more than two sides). So Synod members met in the Hoare Memorial Hall at Church House, Westminster. The Bishop decided that there would be a Eucharist after the debate as a focal point of unity among the voting halves: the House of Bishops, the House of Clergy and the House of Laity.

Prebendary Donald Barnes, a member of the General Synod and Vicar of St Peter's, Belize Park, opened the debate in which Elizabeth Mills, a member of the General Synod, presented a passionate case against the legislation. Many national religious affairs correspondents attended. But the night was in many ways an anticlimax, an overture to the various positions that would be taken for years to come after the final vote at General Synod was taken.

Hope took the opportunity of generally encouraging women's ministry as he had in the Diocese of Wakefield. It was simply ordination to the episcopate and priesthood that posed for him residual questions of authority and decision-making. Hope reflects:

> I think people on the whole knew my position. First of all, a bishop has a particular responsibility for holding the diocese together over an issue when there is a division in the Church and therefore I attempted to ensure that both sides had equal opportunity to give voice to their views whenever I met them. I tried to make sure that my own views were not disproportionately emphasized on one side, as it were, against another. I have tried to ensure an openness of debate.

The vote went as expected with the focus inevitability on how David Hope had voted. Leonard, who was possibly already thinking about a life in the Roman Catholic Church where he would in the future serve as a priest, voted against. The voting was:

House of Bishops:	For 0	Against 3	Abstentions 1
House of Clergy:	For 45	Against 57	Abstentions 1
House of Laity:	For 45	Against 51	Abstentions 3

Hope had abstained, London was against. He issued a statement reflecting his growing confidence:

Tonight's vote means that all 44 dioceses have now voted on the draft legislation. The vote of the Diocese of London will be considered alongside the other dioceses of the Church of England before members of the General Synod take a final vote next year. As this process continues, and as I said in my speech during the course of the debate, it is our Christian duty to support, care for and pray for each other and to extend a real and genuine courtesy to one another.

Hope's first London Christmas as Bishop turned out to be a memorable one. He was naturally pleased to be in St Paul's Cathedral at the heart of the nation's worship on the most holy night of the year. The *Evening Standard*, whose interest in church issues throughout the 1990s was largely limited to frequent broadsides from its columnist, A. N. Wilson, surprisingly asked Hope to write an op-ed (comment) piece for the Christmas Eve edition. Hope focused on the common theme of children at Christmas, and on memories of Christmas in Bucharest under Ceausescu. He also made reference to the recent spate of terrorist attacks which affected the psyche of London in a big way in the early 1990s, as the Irish question continued to produce bomb scare after bomb scare and the occasional direct attack from Irish Nationalists.

'Disruptions to travel and transport as well as the creation of a general atmosphere of fear and unease which such incidents create do gnaw away at us, despite the real resilience and fortitude of the British spirit,' he wrote. Hope called for a real Christmas spirit: 'The gift of Jesus Christ, God's gift to us of himself, is a timely call to us once again this Christmas tide that our capital city has so much potential and so many possibilities, yet for the real human being to flourish, each one of us has something to contribute; ourselves and our own determination that the goodwill and kindness and generosity of the Christmas spirit should be taken forward actively and into the weeks and months ahead.'

The edition of *Heart of the Matter* featuring David Hope was screened on 9 February 1992. Questions of authority and decision-making dominated the programme. Hope admitted to 'some residual hesitations about the principle of the ordination of women to the ministerial priesthood. Even in terms of Anglican Communion, one cannot yet say that there is a substantial mind of the Church to make it right to make this move towards women priests at this particular juncture. That's why I cannot accept the legislation as it presently stands.'

The Bishop affirmed the ministry of women, both lay and ordained, and refused to be drawn on his own future plans if the legislation, as seemed likely, gained adequate support in the General Synod. 'It is no help now to start pronouncing on what I will do and what I won't do. It is very important that we go on with the process. As the process moves along I need to reflect on the decisions that are being made and come to a mind on what I may or may not do.'

Human sexuality was another key theme of the programme. Responding to discussions in the Church on the question of sexuality, Hope wanted to be affirming: 'I think there is a considerable degree of homophobia about not only in the Church but in society more generally. Christians ought to be affirming the value and dignity of each and every human being created in the image and likeness of God. Wherever that individual is within the spectrum of sexuality that dignity and decorum ought to be recognized and affirmed.'

The Bishop reminded clergy watching the programme of the question asked of them at the time of their ordination about the fashioning and framing of their lives 'according to the way of Christ'. He went on: 'There are clear and high standards expected of sacrifice and discipline on the part of homosexual and heterosexual clergy.'

As Hope's new Press Secretary (this was the first year I worked for him) and London Diocesan Communications Officer, I was kept out of diocesan politics. I never once attended Bishop's Staff Meeting or Bishop's Council but was always debriefed by Chaplain Tim Thornton. I was close, yet distant. Hope trusted my judgement but had his own clear mind. He was shrewd in keeping me up to date with potential, problematic news stories, telling me just enough in advance to enable me to prepare a satisfactory response while not becoming overexcited about many issues that never saw the light of day. Having established a successful tabloid newspaper for the Diocese of Bradford (*Newsround*), Hope asked me to do the same for the Diocese of London. I founded *The London Link* and set about securing advertising and sponsorship for 55,000 copies, published four times a year, at no cost to the parishes apart from my time spent on the paper. The first edition appeared at Easter 1992 and Hope was pleased with the result, acknowledging that the tabloid style could not fail but attract a majority of readers. There was criticism of the newspaper ('blunt', 'crude', 'raw') after its launch at St Bride's, Fleet Street, but a lot of support too. The first issue led on a £4 million new church project at Brentford, but there was also coverage of Bishop Hope's Lenten series of addresses from the steps of the Royal Exchange, which had introduced him to the City, and pictures of the Bishops of London, Southwark (Roy Williamson) and Chelmsford (John Waine) preparing for a helicopter ride over the Docklands development.

In his first episcopal column the Bishop urged readers: 'We need to be reaching out with love into our community.' An article by Leigh Hatts introducing Richard Chartres, the new Bishop of Stepney, was headlined 'Yes, I was expelled from the cubs but the pickled onion incident was greatly exaggerated.' *The London Link* died in 2003, but it had ten good years and reinvigorated a sense of diocese.

Hope's first two key appointments of Richard Chartres to Stepney and Graham Dow to Willesden proved effective. On the one hand he provided the diocese with his own successor in Chartres, while in Graham Dow, a vicar from the Coventry Diocese, London welcomed a priest with a strong mind and a clear commitment to evangelism and renewal as well as a deep respect for spirituality within the charismatic tradition.

The worst of the IRA attacks on London occurred in April 1992 when a large bomb ripped through Bishopsgate in the heart of the City and the tiny, beautiful church of St Ethelburga was almost completely destroyed. Keen to show his resolution and support for City workers and the City of London as a whole, Hope visited the scene of devastation. There was nowhere more poignant and moving that day than the rubble of St Ethelberga's. Wearing a hard hat and stumbling through the debris, Hope declared that the church would be rebuilt as a sign of peace and reconciliation after such brutality and hatred. Today, the church is just that.

Hope's greatest lasting legacy to the diocese was an initiative launched in June 1992 which he called 'Agenda for Action', consisting of a Mission Action Plan for the eight years leading up to the millennium at diocesan, deanery and parish level. Such an initiative, involving each and every parish, was unheard of. It was a subtle, radical strategy but, because of his premature departure to become Archbishop of York in 1995, it was also Hope's greatest example of unfinished business. The agenda focused on two key words in the task of mission: *priorities* – what priorities does the Church have for the future?, and *resources* – what, in the way of people, buildings and finance, could the Church offer the wider community in partnership with others? He gave three couplets – prayer and worship, teaching and service, care and service – for parishes to consider.

'Agenda for Action' was well received. It was aimed, *The Times* suggested, at reducing the terrible decline in churchgoing in London (nationally 24 out of every 1,000 people go to church, in London the figure is 16). Hope asked each priest to discuss the questions of priorities and resources and to send their Mission Action Plan (or MAP) to him personally so that it could be discussed by bishop and parish in the future. The *Church of England Newspaper*, on the front page of its 12 June edition, summarized the thrust of 'Agenda for Action': 'Parishes to be linked in clusters, with some merging and others being designated mission areas, and a rethink on clergy deployment.'

At the same time, Hope somewhat controversially took the opportunity of grasping the nettle of the City churches. He announced the Templeman Commission, under the chairmanship of Lord Templeman, whose task was to make recommendations about how the 36 City churches could fit into the diocese as a whole. It was a mammoth task. Hope sent a pastoral letter to every church in the diocese one month before the inevitable vote on women priests calling for 'a real courtesy and patient charity' towards those who had different views. 'It is important that all of us – our difference in this and other matters notwithstanding – do all we can to remain in love and charity with our neighbours.' The Bishop also announced that a celebration of the Eucharist would take place on Thursday 29 October, which would pray for the guidance of the Holy Spirit, and for the unity of the Church. 'Whichever way the vote goes, there are bound to be those who will be greatly distressed and some will be considering their position within the Church of England. If either myself or members of the senior staff, bishops and archdeacons, can be of any help or assistance to you, then we shall be available and make a priority in our diaries to give time to those who wish to discuss further their concerns,' wrote Hope with real passion and concern.

Many were sceptical about how such an opponent of women's ordination could be so conciliatory, but that would be part of the burden of Hope's ministry. On the evening before the vote, Hope went to a vigil at Westminster Abbey as well as spending time in his own private chapel in London House. The weight of the occasion was beginning to affect him: 'I was conscious that whichever way the vote went there would still be a continuing ministry of healing and reconciliation because it was well known that it was going to be a very close vote indeed. Whatever the result, there were going to be a substantial number of people who would be unhappy.' He walked the very short walk to Church House with Bishop Roy Williamson. He had worked hard on his speech. The usual pressure groups had assembled outside Church House with their banners, leaflets and posters. BBC television was to screen the debate live on BBC2. 'I think most people were just relieved that the day of decision had arrived. There was a feeling of "Let's get on with it", and people were being extremely civil and understanding,' says Hope.

He sat in his normal place in the Synod and expected to be called early in the debate. He was the acknowledged leader of the opposition. The Archbishop of York chaired the session. The Bishop of Guilford, Michael Aidie, proposed the legislation. By now, the arguments both for and against were so well known it was difficult to find something original to say. During a speech by David Silk, Archdeacon of Leicester, a fire alarm went off and proceedings were suspended. Some saw that as a great irony. Then Hope was called:

I am not, nor ever have been, one of those who believe that it is impossible for a woman to be ordained . . . But today's debate is about a certain legislative package, a series of proposals to put into effect the ordination of women to the priesthood. It is here that I am considerably more certain that this legislation has not got it right; in fact, I have strong hesitations and reservations about its aims, tone and possible effects on the Church of England . . . I submit that if this legislation is passed, the Church of England will be very different indeed and those unable to accept this new theological understanding with theological and ecclesiastical integrity will inevitably and increasingly find themselves ignored and marginalized. Having said this, I shall try to respect with as good and

generous a grace as I can whatever decision is reached at the end of
the day, praying that God will indeed give me the necessary grace
and wisdom to continue in communion and fellowship with all in
my diocese whatever their views, and I hope and pray they with me
also.

Hope received loud applause from all Synod members. There was
relief at the lack of bitterness. But Archbishop Carey and Bishop Roy
Williamson had still to speak and, deep down, Hope knew that the
vote was swinging in favour of the legislation. Carey thanked Hope
for his speech. He then gave a clear and honest summary of where he
stood on the issue, and why. He said that progress had been made
slowly:

> I urge those who see the future only in terms of schism to recog-
> nize that disputes about the nature of ministry are not regarded in
> the New Testament as grounds for formal separation from one's
> fellow Christians. The step I hope we shall take today is a develop-
> ment of the Church's tradition. The ordination of women to the
> priesthood alters not a word in the creeds, the scriptures or the
> faith of our Church.

There was a lunch break. Carey chaired the afternoon session.
Williamson's speech won the afternoon: 'I genuinely and completely
respect the views of others in this Synod and I speak only for myself
when I say that I cannot with any degree of integrity challenge the
injustices of society and turn a blind eye to the apparent injustice in
the Church which prevents women from testing their vocation to the
priesthood.' The Bishop of Durham, David Jenkins, said a 'No' vote
would condemn the Church of England to five years of wasted energy.
After an exhausting day the Synod voted:

House of Bishops:	For 39	Against 13
House of Clergy:	For 176	Against 74
House of Laity:	For 169	Against 82

Hope remembers the moment of the vote:

I knew that it was going to be a 'Yes' vote when I returned to my seat. The atmosphere told me that it had just squeezed through. It was an intuitive feeling. I also knew from the moment of the vote being read out that we were in for some tough times ahead. Life would never be quite the same again. After the Archbishop read out the result no one around me said anything at all. I remained in the chamber for the next vote on the canon.

That evening the Bishop of London was attending a service at St Martin in the Fields. It is hard to remember the different feelings and emotions which particularly affected the opponents of the legislation, but Hope has an abiding memory: 'The thing that really put me off happened as I left, when a couple of women deacons saw me passing and one of them, in a loud rather bitter voice said, "The sooner they get out now the better." That really did stick in my gullet. I have no idea who they were. It was an unpleasant, ungenerous and ungracious comment.' A few months after the vote, Hope collaborated with me in a series of interviews looking back over events which resulted in the ordination of women (*Never the Same Again: A Journey Through Women's Ordination*, with the Bishop of London. Darton, Longman and Todd, 1993). The book had a low print run, was produced quickly, but had a surprising impact. Many said they simply did not realize what Hope had been through as the vote approached and immediately afterwards.

He told me this: 'This is a very lonely job. I suppose that's what you have to expect at the top in a situation like this. But just at the moment I feel as if I'm at the bottom.'

Following the 11 November vote, the Bishop of London came under increasing pressure to satisfy the demands of those who wanted to exclude women priests from his diocese on the one hand and those who were urging him to ordain them on the other. Threats and intimidation came from both sides and David Hope felt isolated and alone. The very reason for the appointment of Hope to the See of London would now become apparent. As a way forward, the Bishop was to be the focus of unity: 'A bishop has a particular responsibility for holding a diocese together over any issue where there is division within the Church, and I have tried to interpret the understanding of one side to the other.'

His early spadework of listening paid off. Despite his personal opposition, supporters of women priests in general respected and supported him: 'I had a meeting after the vote with all the women deacons in the diocese and tried to explain to them what the situation was as I saw it. It was a tense and difficult meeting. A possibility existed that they would not be ordained in the Diocese of London and that was obviously a cause of great concern to them.'

Hope found no shortage of support for the ordination of women. Frequently he was told that because a parish's woman deacon was excellent he should have no hesitation about ordaining women to the priesthood. A series of meetings with the Deans of Women's Ministry in the diocese took on a high priority in his diary. But it was the opponents who were angry and grieving for their church. 'Forward in Faith' was born in the heart of Hope's diocese, on 25 November 1992. He did not attend, but was briefed on what happened. He liked the title adopted by the group but was concerned that they took a realistic line as to the options available to them.

Then came news that the Australian General Synod had also voted in favour of women priests, two days after the inauguration of 'Forward in Faith'. The pressure and anger were mounting. David Londin will not forget Advent 1992. It was his lowest spiritual point as a Bishop. He looked tired, drawn. In lighter moments he said he dreamed of being a cashier at Tesco or of any job which he could 'leave at five'.

Morale among the clergy and laity of the diocese was low. Hundreds of laity were pondering their future. Many priests considered quitting. The media coverage was pessimistic and grim, particularly from the more Catholic elements. Hope wondered what he might do. The voting figures at the London Diocesan Synod 12 months before the General Synod vote were a constant reminder of the strength of opposition in London. There were immediate calls for separate post-ordination training courses. More threatening was the postbag: 'What, Bishop Hope, are you going to do?' By December, 'Forward in Faith' was obviously pulling a lot of practical, moral and financial support from the Diocese of London. Hope kept a central line on the issue. To the admiration of some and the sheer frustration of others (many of whom felt let down by him) the Bishop of London tried to keep the differing factions together and to come up with a watertight plan which would protect all integrities.

John Habgood, then Archbishop of York, realized the pickle Hope was in far more than George Carey. Habgood's support for a rescue plan for opponents was critical in these months. Hope believes Habgood's leadership of the Church of England alongside Robert Runcie and George Carey has been vastly underestimated. It is rare to find one Archbishop of York who paints such a glowing tribute to his direct predecessor, but it is clear that Hope believes Habgood mopped up many of the issues left behind by both Archbishops of Canterbury he served:

> John is a hugely underestimated person. Throughout the time he was at Bishopthorpe, John Habgood was always there to rescue the House of Bishops. He was the one who would come in and propose a compromise – an appropriate way forward. He could always sum up extremely well where we had got to and gather the mind. Also, and it has been vastly underplayed, is the fundamental spirituality of John Habgood. It really was immense – a huge humility which is compelling and attractive. When I went to see John Habgood shortly before I came to York he gave me two pieces of advice. 'You are running a long-distance race – not the 100 metres sprint. And learn to be a lazy Archbishop.' I now know what he meant.

Discussions across the river with Bishop Roy Williamson, in the Diocese of Southwark, led to the emergence of what became known as the London Plan. Both dioceses contained supporters and opponents of women priests. One bishop was in favour, another was against. Hope allowed the Bishop of Fulham (then, Bishop John Klyberg, a highly amusing and very human pastor) who did not have a territorial area and was opposed to women's ordination, to offer extended episcopal care under the Episcopal Ministry Act of Synod of 1994 to those parishes in the Dioceses of Southwark and Rochester who objected to women priests. In simple terms, he became what was known as a 'flying bishop'. He would carry out confirmations and make episcopal visits. The plan was seen as an excellent resolution. Hope would continue to offer pastoral oversight as Bishop to everyone in his diocese, but he would ordain only deacons. Those

opposed to women priests were safe with him. The Bishop of Southwark and some of his own area bishops could offer support to women
priests and their advocates. It was complicated but it worked. It was a
rescue plan.

Almost without exception, Hope has never ordained a priest since
then – male or female – and this is a matter of continuing sadness and
loss for him. 'There have been two exceptions only, so basically that
has been the price for me. People don't appreciate really when they
talk about the pain of all this that we all have pain, we can all talk
about that.'

Throughout the row over ordination, and with the later divisive
debate on gay clergy, Hope has always sought to act for the good of
the Church.

> I knew that if opponents of women's ordination were to stay in the
> Church after the Synod decision then some action had to be taken
> to help them. Some provision had to be made for them, and I made
> sure I put the London Plan in place before the Act of Synod was
> finally decided, so hopefully that gave some hints as to how the
> thing might be managed.
>
> I was concerned that we should put the good of the Church
> above all this. As I constantly say also over the gay debate – how
> could the Church be seen to be in touch with the gospel of recon-
> ciliation if we were not able to practise what we preached? I
> recognize that some of the arrangements are less than satisfactory,
> but if we are going to live together with respect and courtesy then,
> until the matter was resolved – and it won't be resolved in my
> lifetime – we have to live with a degree of anomaly.

Roy Williamson, now retired and living in Nottingham, remembers those days well. 'It was tough, I can tell you. But I really did
everything I could to make things work not only for the Diocese of
Southwark but also for David Hope. It was strange, eventually taking
that first ordination service in St Paul's Cathedral of all those women.
I did it to ensure that we stayed together in our differences.'

It was announced before Christmas that St Augustine's, Highgate,
had become the first London parish to publicly vote against women
priests exercising any ministry within the parish. That denial of the

right of women to act as priests would be repeated across the diocese. Cardinal Basil Hume, the Catholic Cardinal Archbishop of Westminster, kept in close touch with Hope and was fully supportive, seeing Hope's predicament. He was swamped with enquiries from Anglican lay people and priests who wanted the Roman Catholic Church to offer them a sanctuary so that they could escape from what they saw as unilateral madness. Hume was sympathetic to Hope's plight but aware that his own Church had to come up with answers to questions about priestly vocations from Anglican priests and the vexed issue of married Anglican priests who wanted to pursue a Catholic ministry elsewhere.

Hume travelled to Rome on 29 November for a meeting of European Catholic Bishops at which the ordination of women could hardly be ignored. It was suggested that Hume would meet Cardinal Edward Cassidy, the Pope's Australian-born adviser on ecumenical affairs 'to discuss pleas by senior traditionalists to form their own group within the Roman Catholic Church'. There was the fact that Hope's predecessor, Graham Leonard, was now widely reported to be about to quit the Church of England and become a Roman Catholic. Hope felt even more isolated, and the pressure did not diminish. Leonard, to the surprise and chagrin of many, became a Monsignor within the Roman Catholic Church. Many felt let down and deserted by their former bishop – particularly those who found Hope lacking in the conservatism for which Leonard was most respected.

John Gummer, Agriculture Minister in John Major's government and a fellow Guardian with Bishop David of the Shrine of Our Lady of Walsingham, resigned his membership of the General Synod. Two hundred and fifty evangelicals, opposed to women priests, wrote in protest to Synod.

George Carey was seen by many to have no realization of the real implications of the vote. From retirement he sees Hope's predicament much better than he did from Lambeth Palace. While Lord Carey's stance on women priests may well be considered visionary and radical by some, others saw a narrowness and ecumenical stubbornness and ignorance for which they never forgave him.

Relations, at this time, between Lambeth Palace and Barton Street were not easy. The media sensed this and Hope admitted, off the record, that he was often exasperated and amazed at the mess that had resulted and the lack of sensitivity from Lambeth. But it never seriously soured his personal relationship with Carey and the two would work together as archbishops less than three years later. Ruth Gledhill, religion correspondent of *The Times*, believes that the media breakfasts hosted regularly by Hope as Bishop of London were valuable aids to getting his message across:

> Here was the Bishop of London with all of the journalists, allowing us to ask him absolutely anything about anything. It was new and it was good. Not a question of one-upmanship at all. Hope has never had hostility towards the media. For some bishops, the media is evil – they are frightened to death of it. But not Hope.
>
> Hope had confidence. Confidence to deal with us and the agendas our news desks demanded we supported. I remember, at the news conference when he was to be unveiled as Archbishop, there was elation. Not only that the Church had done this – the right thing – but that a man so honest and down to earth had been given what he truly deserved and what the Church needed. It was because he knew us and we trusted him that we shared the joy of his progression through the hierarchy.

Carey is the first to acknowledge that maybe at the time, as Archbishop of Canterbury, he was not fully in tune with the concerns and fears of the opponents who looked to David Hope for support.

> I know that for a time after the vote, David was in deep despair while I was elated and exhilarated – yet fearful too. I don't think, looking back, I fully understood the great fear felt by the Anglo-Catholics. It seemed that David was saying 'I think this is a wrong turn we have taken and I need to help my Church cope with this; how, now, can we rediscover the Catholic tradition?' David positioned himself carefully and strategically: we can still hold on to those things which are special to us even though we are not totally happy with the way things have turned out.

Hope, of course, lived out this analysis of Dr Carey at first hand and did go through a period of reluctance, anger, frustration and isolation. Journalists reflecting on that time see it very differently. Christopher

Morgan, of the *Sunday Times*, believes that Carey kept Hope out of the loop altogether and remembers a key member of Carey's Lambeth staff telling him that she had 'faxed David Hope and told him to stop speaking out on these issues all the time. How David Hope put up with it, facing all the challenges he did in London, is unclear to me.'

Morgan is frustrated by the Carey years and believes Hope made the best of a bad situation: 'I got the impression that Hope was frustrated by what he saw as Lambeth's inability to deal with the outside world. Carey operated on his own and Hope let him get on with it. He was closer to Habgood than he was to Carey. David was never brought into the loop and, to be honest, never would be completely. He recognized that and lived with it.'

One of the key concerns of David Hope in the mid-1990s was the Conservative Government's desire to relax the laws relating to Sunday trading. While Hope acknowledged the inevitability of the change, he regretted the impact of seven-day working and shopping. He cried out for a day when the streets could relax from the hustle and bustle of the rest of the week and, in a rare appearance in the House of Lords, he told Peers:

> Here is a principle which is not simply just for religious or Christian people, but for individuals and society as a whole. It is for our good and well-being, for our body, mind and spirit; for our cohesion; simply, it is for our very sanity and survival. I suspect that the needs and demands will become the same as any other day. Have we really thought carefully about the knock-on effects of seven-day trading? We shall surely see more people expected to work on Sundays or unable to resist the pressure put upon them by their employers.

This was a rare foray into politics for Hope. He remains uneasy about bishops in parliament – even though he ultimately recognizes that they need to have a voice there:

> I went into the House of Lords as Bishop of London rarely – but as Archbishop of York I would go in hardly ever. There was the diocese, the whole Northern Province and so on, and it was very difficult. I think there should be religious representatives in the

House of Lords and I think bishops should be part of that religious representation. I don't think they should be the only religious representatives and there are many well-qualified lay persons who can represent religious or theological views – indeed, many of them more so than an ordained person.

The first women priests were ordained in the Diocese of London in April 1994, and Hope was in one his darkest moods. Although he had accepted the service in his own cathedral as inevitable, the event marked the culmination of years of anticipation. Media interest was enormous. Bishop Roy Williamson ordained the women, but there was intense speculation as to whether Hope would attend. Even I, as his Press Secretary, did not know if the car would leave. In the end Hope turned up, sitting quietly in his throne, praying for the future unity of God's Church. I travelled with him in the car. We did not exchange a word. There were protests, outside and inside the Cathedral, but the women were, of course, ordained. The sight of the Bishop of London seated in his throne in his own cathedral, unable to take part as people were ordained, marked a new stage in the fracture of the Church of England.

Many Graham Leonard supporters despised Hope for even daring to show up, but the Bishop recognized that his pastoral care could only apply if he at least attended.

On a much more positive note, the Templeman Commission reported in 1994, after 18 months of deliberations, on the pastoral and mission role of the City's churches. It recommended that four City parishes be created; All Hallows by the Tower, St Batholomew the Great, St Giles Cripplegate and St Helen's Bishopsgate, with a further three satellite churches attached to each. Other churches could be put to alternative use. Unfortunately, as with 'Agenda for Action', due to Hope's premature departure to York, the Templeman recommendations were never acted on.

So, Hope was fighting many fires. But he was aware that one other major issue was hovering in the background. The question of homosexuality was to overtake the ordination of women and dominate the agenda, and Hope decided to go public on the very private matter of his own sexuality.

7

An Outrage!

Dr John's withdrawal is a capitulation to homophobia.
(Peter Tatchell)

There is absolutely no doubt that the February 2004 debate on homosexuality at the General Synod of the Church of England marked a significant shift in the Established Church's position on the gay issue.

Suddenly, and without warning, the Synod seemed to be embracing a more inclusive and less judgemental attitude to non-heterosexuals and, from a wide range of speakers representing all traditions, there was an acceptance that the Church had, somehow, to 'get a life' (the words of one speaker quoting his teenage son) and move on.

Just two months earlier, in his 2003 Christmas sermon, ✠David Ebor stressed that the majority of the population could not see what all the fuss was about. Large numbers of regular worshippers in parish churches all over the country simply do not understand why the issue of human sexuality has continued to undermine the national profile of the Church. It is clear that many gay clergy are among the most dedicated priests in the Church. Some have enjoyed lasting, long-term relationships and most bishops are at least aware of this. Lay gay members of the Church also find the continuous focus on the issue of their sexuality intrusive and ridiculous.

Some of the main reasons homosexuality remains an issue are: a desire by gay rights protestors to ensure equality for clergy and laity; the interest in the story from the media; and the unease and obvious pain felt by some evangelicals about the incompatibility of genital sexual relations between people of the same sex.

Outrage! and the Lesbian and Gay Christian Movement have been at the forefront of a bold attempt to ensure that the Church faces up to sexual equality and overt discrimination, through the questionable tactics of personal 'outings', disruption of services and an invasion of the General Synod. There had been long periods of quiet since 1979 when the Bishop of Gloucester produced a report suggesting that homosexual relations, in some cases, might be morally acceptable, but the issue had never gone away.

The *Guardian*, the *Independent*, *The Times* and the *Daily Telegraph* have each treated the story in a manner reflecting their own particular politics and ethos. Around the time that June Osborne chaired a 1986 working party, which produced a report (never published) on gay clergy, evangelicals began a campaign to make their feelings felt. A General Synod private member's motion presented by Revd Tony Higton (then of Chelmsford Diocese) called on it to reaffirm that 'fornication, adultery, and homosexual acts are sinful'. The Bishop of Chester provided an amendment, which said that homosexual genital acts fall short of the ideal – the ideal being a permanent married relationship – which was carried, but the unease of the Church was clear.

In the early days of the Lesbian and Gay Christian Movement, ably and effectively led by Revd Richard Kirker, the whole Church seemed to be against them. The relationship between LGCM and more militant, secular gay rights organizations such as Outrage! has never been clear. When David Hope became Bishop of London the clamour for a proper debate was gathering momentum. An acute sense of hypocrisy (bishops were ordaining men without asking obvious questions simply because *they* had never been asked) seemed to increase as society became more liberal and it was somehow fashionable to be gay and 'out'. In the police, health service, teaching and the civil service, gender discrimination was illegal. The very generation which the Church of England was struggling to attract – the 18–30s – was likely to turn its back on any organization which did not accept everyone, regardless of race, gender or sexual orientation.

Outrage! began a campaign to 'out' ten bishops in November 1994, naming them at the doors of Church House, Westminster as Synod members arrived. There was a strong rumour that David Hope, the most senior Diocesan Bishop, was on the list. In fact he was not, but there remained the suggestion that his name might be the next one added. Between November 1994 and March 1995, Hope endured one of the worst experiences of his personal and professional life, as Outrage! wrote letters to him couched in confrontational terms, and he responded as best he could. Single and celibate, Hope was aware of rumours that he was gay and that there had been frequent suggestions that x or y was a partner. Being celibate, he became angry and anxious about the rumour mill. He feared for the future of platonic friendships and recognized that as the Bishop of London he had to be incredibly careful as Outrage! began communications with him.

The first year of Rowan Williams' time in Lambeth Palace was overshadowed by the gay issue. Gay rights protestors invaded General Synod, evangelicals were up in arms and the media had a field day. Roy Hattersley, writing in the *Mail on Sunday*'s Night & Day supplement, suggested that Hope had become another victim of what one of his canons described as the 'church's stumbling attempts to come to terms with the twentieth century'.

To this day, the story of what happened between Hope and Outrage! has never been told in full. Hope believes that from the moment he arrived in the capital there were people within the Church hierarchy, lay and ordained, who had him in their sights. 'I know who they are,' he would say, 'don't you worry!' He found it all exasperating, but as coming, to some extent, with the territory. 'It is part of what leading up front is in any walk of life; you are put up to be shot down, and I realized where much of this was coming from.'

Hope also recognizes that his very private lifestyle probably encouraged gossip when he was Principal of St Stephen's House, and perhaps even more so as Vicar of All Saints, Margaret Street. The Anglican Catholic community has a clear, celebrated camp dimension to it, which is paradoxically one of its greatest strengths (it is a reflection of the fact that it does not take itself too seriously) but it is also true that this community was prone to gossip, jealousy and insecurity – not least since women priests were ordained.

Hope had become an exception to the rule: he was a rare top Catholic player in an increasingly Protestant church. To many, he was a throwback to those pioneering missionary priests who celebrated the Gospel in word and sacrament from a Catholic perspective. Many loved him, but some loathed him. Others were simply jealous. The rumours continued, and those disaffected priests and laity who had the ear of activists were sure that Hope could be damaged if it was proved that he was gay.

After the ten bishops had been outed, Peter Tatchell wrote Hope a 'private' letter. He delivered it by hand 'to save embarrassment in the event of it being opened and read by assistants'. Hope agreed to see Tatchell and receive the letter. Tatchell told Hattersley, in his *Mail on Sunday* article, that the two men then had 'a long and helpful discussion'. Hope read the letter again later that night. There were sections in which Tatchell described the prejudices from which gay men suffer before he turned his spotlight on Hope himself. 'Although Outrage! had been passed a lot of detailed information about your personal life which would have enabled us to confidently name you on 30 November, we chose not to do so.' It did not take Hope long to realize that the writing was on the wall and that the focus would soon turn on him. He had no idea what, if any, personal information they had on him: 'I kept thinking that night – who is accusing me? . . . what can they be alleging? To be honest, after the schism over women priests, I had almost had enough at that point.'

Hope decided that he needed some time to reflect on his next move. On Friday 11 March, I accompanied him on a day trip on the new Eurostar train from London Waterloo to Paris. The sole purpose was to discuss the key issue on his mind. He considered a range of options and wanted to discuss them with me as his Press Secretary. Being Hope and loving trains, he enjoyed the new experience of going through the Channel Tunnel and, as the train emerged in France, he became more relaxed, pleased to be away from the hothouse of the diocese. 'I am not prepared to live my life like this, I can tell you,' he kept repeating. It was a confident and resolute refrain. Hope made his way straight to Notre Dame where, it being the middle of Lent, a priest was leading the stations of the cross in colourful French. Hope joined in the service and absorbed the depth of what the priest was saying about sacrifice, suffering, injustice and glory. He was deep in prayer. I studied the face of the priest, a somewhat gloomy man but full of God's grace, totally oblivious to the fact that among the 15 people in his congregation was the Lord

Bishop of London, looking for the strength to do what he had to do. After stations and Mass, Hope found a bistro and ordered the *plat du jour*. By the time the train left for Waterloo, late in the afternoon, Hope had agreed that he would quash the rumours and innuendo on Monday morning with an unprecedented media conference at which the letter from Tatchell and Outrage! would be presented, together with Hope's reply.

He would challenge Outrage! to prove what they were alleging – to put up or shut up. Further, he would not allow a pressure group within the gay community to hold the Church hostage over the gay issue and, even more significantly, to dictate what he said about himself. Hope took legal advice at the highest level. He also consulted Eric Shegog, then Director of Communications for the Church of England. The media were called to a conference by telephone late on the Sunday evening. Some asked if he was to come out, others if he was going to quit. Over 20 journalists turned up. Hope was accompanied by David Faull, Diocesan Registrar, Nigel Seed (now QC), and Eric Shegog. I chaired the meeting. Hope read a prepared statement expressing several months of angst, frustration and hurt and the journalists were presented with the correspondence. Some were writing their stories as others were asking questions. Even the late Betty Saunders, the doyen of ecclesiastical correspondents, looked amazed. Mike Wooldridge, BBC Religious Affairs Correspondent and now World Affairs Correspondent, was staggered when he read the letters: 'We didn't realize David was putting up with this kind of thing,' he said outside London House.

The range of supplementaries – questions which journalists always ask after an official statement – was predictable:

'So you are not gay?'

'How long have you been celibate?'

'Have you ever had a relationship with anyone?'

The possible answers to such questions had been discussed both in Paris and with the legal team. Questions flowed freely about the Church, sexuality as a whole, gays – but then came the question which Hope answered openly and without equivocation: 'But Bishop, if you were not celibate, how would you actually describe your sexuality?' I imagine everyone expected the Bishop either to stall ('It's none of your bloody business') or say something modish such as 'I would be bisexual.' Instead, Hope said: 'I would have to describe my sexuality as a grey area.'

David Faull looked shocked, Eric Shegog turned a whiter shade of pale and Nigel Seed uttered something like 'Good, well that's it Rob I think.' In other words: 'Conference over.' The journalists had their soundbite.

The Bishop of London had denounced Tatchell and Outrage!. He had confirmed his single, celibate life and made it clear that in the context of a celibate lifestyle his sexuality was of no business to anyone but God. Waiting to see how the media responded was excruciating. The BBC's *Nine O'clock News* that night led on the story. Anne Hope remembers the sense of shock and disbelief when a friend rang up to say that the gay rights' group had gone for her twin brother. As with all families, particularly close-knit Yorkshire folk, matters of sexuality are rarely, if ever, discussed: 'David really didn't say too much at the time. It was such big news – that was what amazed all of us! He seems to cope with things like that. He just gets on with the work. We felt for him and respected him even more within the family.'

The media coverage was almost totally supportive of Hope – a fact which Tatchell still finds frustrating. It was obvious that Outrage! had been taken by surprise because Hope had not finally agreed to the conference until late on the Sunday. In a statement, Tatchell fumed: 'At his press conference, the Bishop alleged that he had been forced to make his confession by "intimidatory" pressure from Outrage!. This ridiculous allegation was, indeed, the way the story was reported, even though journalists were shown the friendly, ongoing correspondence between myself and the Bishop, which clearly suggested otherwise. Dr Hope even invited me to tea at his official residence.'

Tatchell betrays a surprising ignorance of Hope's character. Politely, Hope replied to each letter which came to him in London House; he even offered hospitality to Tatchell but, convinced that this dialogue was getting him nowhere, Hope made the decision to publish the letters and let the public decide. Tatchell might describe the correspondence as 'friendly', Hope could not. So Tatchell turned his frustration on the journalists themselves: 'The way journalists self-righteously denounced the "outing" of Dr Hope, which they helped instigate, was bare-faced hypocrisy. Ignoring the facts, the media connived with Dr Hope to depict me as "an enemy of the people" (*Daily Express*) and the Bishop a persecuted innocent.'

In a page-long rant against the journalists who 'supported' Dr Hope, Tatchell suggests: 'And why, if the Bishop had nothing to hide, did his lawyer demand to know what information I had about his personal life? Journalists should have asked these questions, but they didn't. Instead, the media sought to demonise myself and undermine Outrage!'s credibility.' The newspapers began an immediate search for a sexual relationship or friendship between Hope and any partner, woman or man. The press office was inundated with queries from both tabloids and broadsheets. That there was no such partner meant that the story was a non-starter. The press poured its venom on Tatchell: the *Sunday Times* branded him 'the enemy within' and 'public enemy number one'. The *Evening Standard* compared him with 'pure poison'. Sir Bernard Ingham, in the *Daily Express*, suggested Tatchell should be castrated, and Allan Massie in the *Daily Telegraph* that he might become the target of an assassin. Tatchell complained that TV news bulletins failed to take action to hide his personal telephone number on the correspondence, and the BBC banned live interviews with him or any member of Outrage!. Hattersley suggested that Hope's press conference was 'a brilliant tactical stroke'.

David Faull now reflects that 14 March marked a change in Hope: 'I think until that time David was fair but not unduly sympathetic to gay people. He couldn't put up with people fussing about gay relationships and that kind of thing. It wasn't something he really wanted to understand. But I think, once he had decided to say what he did, and I admired him for it, he moved a lot. He became more sympathetic.'

Ruth Gledhill remembers the episode as one of the most dramatic times in her early years as a religious affairs correspondent. She believes that the way Hope handled Tatchell tells us a lot about him, and that Tatchell didn't understand the qualities and nature of the man he took on.

David Hope has always given me the impression that he would have been more at home in a monastery or a parish than as a bishop or archbishop because he is holy – a holy man. He has a totally pastoral heart. Tatchell did himself more harm than he could ever do to Hope because he picked the wrong man. Hope should never have been targeted. There is no hypocrisy or dishonesty in him at all. Tatchell, therefore, was wide of the mark. He lacked understanding of his target and took no notice whatsoever of what stands out from Hope more than anything, and that is his sense of vocation.

In the weeks after the controversy, Hope benefited from a massive amount of support. At times, he considered resignation and a return to the parochial ministry, simply as a protest against the shallowness and 'evil' he had encountered. Most of the time he felt a sense of relief – not out of any weakness, but that his own life and lifestyle had given him enough strength to go on and look to the future with confidence. Soon after this episode, speculation was rife that Hope would be translated to York. He dismissed it out of hand.

Peter Tatchell, whose own profile has been transformed in recent years, partly because he has bravely taken up important but neglected causes (his protests about the regime of Robert Mugabe in Zimbabwe for example) has a clearly different interpretation of what went on with the Church of England. In a well-argued article – 'Media Mendacity Over Outing' – in the *British Journalism Review* (June, 1998) Tatchell questioned the journalists' response to his attempts to put gay rights at the top of the agenda. Writing about the outing campaign, he says: 'It was not an attack on anyone's homosexuality. Our aim was to expose church hypocrisy and defend the homosexual community against bishops who endorse anti-gay discrimination. Because the bishops' homophobia and double standards impact on the lives of other people, the contradiction between their official pronouncements and their personal behaviour was, therefore, a matter of legitimate public interest.' But the situation is obviously not that black and white.

Tatchell should not be expected to understand the checks and balances which allow the Church to function on a day-to-day basis. The Church needs norms and standards but has to deal with the reality of people's lives. Corporate responsibility in the House of Bishops will always be tempered not by hypocrisy or deception but by pastoral needs which arise in the day-to-day ministry of bishops in their dealing with people who need guidance and encouragement towards a more acceptable form of behaviour. For instance, while the bishops as a house may have been opposed to, or cautious about, lowering the age of consent for gay sex from 21 to 18, that is not to say that several bishops would have a greater degree of sympathy for the option than others. But, as in politics, corporate responsibility would demand loyalty to the party line. After Hope's press conference, he has never bothered about what people might be saying about his personal life. His language is stronger and his courage fortified. Though he still doubts such an assessment of his own situation, there is absolutely no question in the minds of many close friends that after March 1995, Hope gradually became more confident, less worried, as if a weight had been lifted from his shoulders.

The very mention of Outrage! or Tatchell would still produce anger and resentment but he had nothing to hide and would enjoy being himself. Hope had always given as much human and spiritual support to gay people as he was able. Their sexuality was not usually an issue: Hope would deal with them as people, without discrimination. Many gay clergy and laity have spoken of how warmly and supportively he had helped them through difficulties and personal problems. One recently said to me: 'David Hope has been amazing to me and my partner. When he was ill David was the first to ask how he was and went out of his way to show pastoral care as a Father in God.'

Hope was strengthened in this ministry too. Then, for several years, homosexuality took a back seat on the synodical agenda. For most of the decade leading up to the millennium, the big issues were liturgical reform, war and peace, and the question of the future of the Anglican communion. This was party due to the fact that the Archbishop of Canterbury, George Carey, succeeded in making it a non-issue, sometimes by simply pleading ignorance. There was a famous episode one Easter Day when Tatchell decided to climb into the pulpit with George Carey in Canterbury to disrupt his Easter address. At the same time, Chris Smith became Culture Secretary in the new Labour Government and was joined by other openly gay colleagues both in Parliament and the Cabinet. There was less discrimination against people on the basis of gender and the lowering of the age of homosexual consent to 18. The whole climate was more pro-gay, although Carey's Church did not embrace this culture.

But the issue would return. With Carey signifying his departure in 2001 and the question of Rowan Williams succeeding him, evangelicals saw clouds gathering on the horizon. Williams had a reputation for empathizing with lesbian and gay people. His inclusive theology and admirable attempts to understand human nature in all its forms were bound to cause problems when translated into Carey's Church. But Hope, in the early part of 2002, was clear: 'This issue will have to be dealt with because it is simmering again, and once George has gone all hell will be let loose if we are not careful.'

However, the way events unfolded in the first year of Williams's archiepiscopate possibly surprised even the most hardened sceptic, and brought Tatchell and Hope face to face for the first time since their meeting in London House almost a decade earlier. Jeffrey John, Canon Missioner at Southwark Cathedral, was unexpectedly nominated suffragan Bishop of Reading in the Diocese of Oxford by the Bishop of Oxford, Rt Revd Richard Harries. Suddenly, just after Williams' arrival at Lambeth Palace, the Church faced the gay issue in a new, more polarized way. John was open and honest about his sexuality and, though admitting to having been in an active gay relationship in the past, he emphasized that he was now in a celibate partnership with another person of the same sex. This was to be an enormous bait to both the media and evangelicals while the liberal and gay traditionalist camps looked on with horror.

Hope smelt serious trouble.

This story unfolded slowly. The key players in 2003 were as follows: Jeffrey John himself; the Archbishop of Canterbury; the Bishop of Oxford; Dr Philip Giddings, a Reader at Greyfriars Church in Reading and a member of Archbishop's Council; the Archbishop of Canterbury's staff; and, of course, the media. After the gradual revelation of John's lifestyle, the media focused on different groups within the Church. Critics of John pointed to public statements and writings on the document *Issues in Human Sexuality* (a paper published by the House of Bishops outlining a policy on all aspects of human sexuality) suggesting that, as a Bishop, John would have difficulty living by what was written there.

Hope himself was worried by this: 'While I have a good deal of respect for Jeffrey, I really was concerned about what he was reported to have said about *Issues* and I suppose I could see that people would have a field day in criticizing a man who would apparently have put into practice something which it had been reported he might find difficult to live with.' John is a known supporter of those who would like to see greater equality for lesbian and gay people and the Bishop of Oxford spoke strongly at his Diocesan Synod urging members not to give in to homophobia. For many (particularly evangelicals) this appointment, regarded as radical by some observers, was premature and ill-advised. Hope's links to John were not at all remote. Hope was John's college Principal at St Stephen's House, and a lecture delivered by John seven years earlier, quoting Hope as being supportive of a gay lifestyle, was now dragged on to the news pages.

Hope was livid that a totally private, pastoral conversation with John had been splashed across the press. Even today, he refuses to discuss what was said. Hope adhered to the Church's teaching on homosexuality and he had not diverged from this in the case of John. In the week this furore hit the broadsheets the first openly gay man – a divorced father of two – was elected as a bishop in the US and the newspapers eagerly sought Rowan Williams' views: Was he pleased? Where was the Church going? Would Williams survive long-term?

Hope had a grim weekend and a grimmer week. It had been some time since he was so downhearted. He again contemplated early retirement, and later he summarized his feelings on the issue:

What is the point in doing what you have to do to help people, people who take you into their confidence and you into theirs, only to see your words used as political fodder in a totally different context? Of course it is part of the job – but it is one, quite frankly, which I will not miss at all.

The Jeffrey John saga was a new departure, a new level of disunity: too little listening and too much shouting. It worries me, and because it affects people's lives it causes me great concern. Looking back over it now, and at the events which affected me personally much earlier as Bishop of London, I am worried by the Church's preoccupation with an issue which to most people is obviously important, private, but not the be-all and end-all of our *raison d'être*.

It was so serious that, as his Press Secretary, I returned from a planned 12-day holiday in Spain after just five days. The 2003 General Synod of the Church of England in York was predictably dominated by the fallout of the John saga. This time, Tatchell decided to invade Synod and protest in front of everyone. Security at the University of York was appallingly lax. When David Hope saw Tatchell march on to the stage it was the first time the two had been in such close proximity for almost a decade and I watched David as the scene unfolded. Synod was disrupted. There was a feeling that the whole issue was getting out of hand, and certainly out of perspective. Many walked out. Many more stayed to hear what Outrage! had to say.

Tatchell looked over to David Hope. Hope looked back. The two Archbishops stayed and listened. 'It would have looked very wrong indeed if we had simply walked out,' Hope said afterwards. Hope realized that the debate had moved on. It was bigger, wider, greater, and not at all personal. The love which had been offered to him from every quarter of the Church was tangible, warm, understanding and totally without qualification. I believe it was a cathartic moment for Hope. 'You know, some of what they are saying we have to hear. The way they are saying it I totally disagree with, but we must listen, we must be courteous, we all have a lot to learn.'

The Evangelical Assembly in Blackpool during September 2003 was similarly afflicted. The coffee shops and corridors were full of people talking about a counter-attack. After Jeffrey John had finally withdrawn or been forced to withdraw (depending on your interpretation of events) his acceptance of the See of Reading in early July 2003, the Dean of Southwark, Colin Slee, called events 'spiritual apartheid'. He said that John had been a 'victim of appalling prejudice'. Peter Tatchell weighed in: 'It is monstrous that the Church of England is allowing its appointments to be dictated by ecclesiastical bigots. Dr John's withdrawal is a capitulation to homophobia.'

Hope looked on. He could hardly believe the extent of the diversion from evangelism, outreach, celebration and ministry. He commented to the Bishop of London in private: 'This is not the Church into which I was ordained.' His official comment on the John withdrawal was more measured: 'The decision of Jeffrey John . . . can bring no pleasure to anyone. There can be no excuse for the way in which almost every aspect of Jeffrey John's life has been subject to the most intrusive scrutiny. I have a deep concern for him in all of this, and want to assure him of my prayers.'

An anonymous gay vicar writing in the *Guardian* on 7 July 2003 summed up what most Anglicans felt at that time: 'Welcome to the demise of the Church of England.' Hope said this: 'It does bother me that so much of my time as a Bishop . . . has been taken up by what or what does not go on in the bedroom and issues related to it.'

As Hope began to prepare for eventual retirement it was clear that he remained vexed, disappointed and sometimes angry, not only at the Church's inability to deal with the issue of sex and sexuality, but also that so many factions within it could press their view at the risk of further damaging church unity. Hope believes the English Church has become caught up in the peculiarly British obsession with sex, the bedroom and the physical. But he did see signs of hope in the later February 2004 Synod debate on human sexuality. He felt the tone was suddenly more positive, more relevant, more real. Perhaps, all that debate, all that time spent, and the personal hurt he had suffered, might have been part of a worthwhile movement towards the resolution of a key issue.

8

Earthquake

I asked David about the Rosary beads he was carrying (he carried them throughout the pilgrimage) and he explained the basics of the Rosary to me. I was fascinated, so he went on to teach me how to pray the Rosary, which I have never forgotten to this day. I was able to use what he taught me and it cheered my spirit. I will never forget it.

(Ruth Gledhill)

Because of the way in which the human sexuality issue gripped the whole Church, and because the fall-out from the ordination of women to the priesthood was really beginning to bite, the departure of David Hope from the Diocese of London to be Primate of England and Archbishop of York is one of the vaguest memories I have of my time working with him.

While speculation that Hope was destined for York was rife, there was still a group of people who probably felt he might not now be able to go, and an even larger and far more significant group who felt that he had not yet finished the job in London. To a certain extent, the latter group was right. Hope's departure was premature. There were many things he could have achieved, had he stayed. Hope's dramatic structural changes and the implementation of a missionary strategy needed more time. 'Agenda for Action' was reaping positive results, and changes to the central administration and financial structure of the Diocese of London were incomplete. But the Crown Appointments Commission, responsible for choosing John Habgood's successor, clearly had Hope in their sights.

Six weeks after Hope's clear-the-air press conference, a journalist called me to say that he had seen David Hope going through the recently erected security gates at the end of Downing Street en route to see Prime Minister Major. I asked Hope outright if he had been in Downing Street the previous night. In an embarrassed voice, he told me not to ask him such direct questions. A couple of weeks later Hope called me, just as he had done when destined to become Bishop of London. He asked me to call round and see him the following morning. For the second time in five years, he showed me a letter from the Prime Minister, this one inviting him to become Archbishop of York, and told me he had accepted. His delight at the appointment was mixed with disappointment that, maybe, things he had wanted to achieve for the Church of England in the capital would not now be realized.

Paradoxically, the press conference announcing his appointment would not be in York, but at Church House, Westminster. In retrospect, this was wrong. I had to lead the march from a preparation room to the media conference and sit alongside Hope. As we entered the room Betty Saunders, putting two and two together, shouted – 'It can't be, it is!', and burst into tears. She said her confidence in the Church of England had been transformed by the appointment of Hope to York after all he had been through that year.

Within an hour, Hope was boarding the train to York, where another large gathering of journalists would question him, for a York-shireman to be moving into Bishopthorpe Palace was a great story. Hope was relaxed and full of vitality. The spring was back in his step. He talked of his immense joy and surprise – and of the great responsibility of succeeding John Habgood.

In the London diocese, quite a few thought that in moving too early Hope had compromized progress. One said the Diocese of London 'resembled a building site' and then asked, 'Who on earth is going to put it back together?' There was a great sense of frustration and immediate speculation as to who would succeed Hope, with Richard Chartres clearly leading the way – along with Alan Chesters, the Bishop of Blackburn.

Hope agreed that one event in his diary would go ahead – a pilgrimage to the Holy Land. He led over 250 pilgrims from across the country around the Holy Land with enormous energy and zeal.

'It's about coming back to the basics of what our faith is all about – what it all really means,' he kept on saying throughout the hectic but enjoyable eight days. He was followed throughout by a BBC crew of Patrick Hargreaves, Cathy Killick and Keith Massey who were preparing a documentary to be shown in November on the eve of his enthronement in York Minster. It was only six months since the Outrage! incident and four weeks to the enthronement itself. It was turning out to be quite a year.

Hope personally devised the pilgrimage programme. The group would travel north from Ben Gurion Airport, Tel Aviv to Tiberias (via Nazareth and Cana) before taking the West Bank road to Jerusalem. Rene Siva had spent months preparing what was, for him, a flagship tour along with the help of Hadera-based guide Leon Segal and his wife Etty who had become personal friends of the new Archbishop. Leon, in Israel, was proud of his friendship with David Hope and told many of his other pilgrim groups of his archiepiscopal associations. The title of the pilgrimage was 'Following Jesus Today'.

Hope went on ahead to the Crown Plaza Hotel, Tel Aviv, where he had a magnificent view over the Mediterranean Sea. A rather precarious balcony, with a dramatic drop to a concrete promenade below, ensured that his nightly aperitif of whisky was always consumed with one hand gripping his glass and the other the balcony rail. Both the Palestinians and the Israelis went out of their way to make the group welcome. These were glorious days of pure relaxation, totally unheard of outside the traditional August holiday which Hope enjoys every year. The new Primate even ventured to taste his first-ever fast food, only to find that he had to read the Burger King menu in Hebrew: he ended up with a Double Whopper and chips, declining the Coca-Cola and setting off instead to the pub next door for a glass of red wine.

His group took the overnight flight from Heathrow and the idea was that Hope would be waiting for them outside the group arrivals meeting hall. He had six air-conditioned Volvo coaches all with 'Diocese of London' printed on both front and back windows. It was all rather strange, as he had just moved to York. Hope greeted each pilgrim in turn with real enthusiasm, asking them alternately if they had had a good flight, slept at all and welcoming them to the Holy Land. For many it had been their first plane journey, others could hardly believe they were there.

The first day was exhausting. The whole party visited Nazareth and Cana of Galilee, without any further sleep. A team of ordained and lay leaders looked after each coach and Hope hopped regularly from one bus to another to travel a part of the pilgrimage with a different group each day. There was a feeling of excitement and expectation when they arrived at the Church of the Annunciation and Hope reminded them of the visit of the Angel Gabriel to this small crater-like town in Upper Galilee. Then it was on to Tiberias, by the Sea of Galilee, where the group was to spend two nights. The highlights of the northern part of the tour were a boat trip on the Sea of Galilee where Hope led a meditation 'Peace, Be Still'. Then it was up to the summit of the Mount of Beatitudes on a balmy and bright November day, for a full open-air Eucharist on the sayings of Jesus in the Sermon on the Mount. Just as a pilgrim read the words 'Blessed are the peacemakers, for theirs is the Kingdom of Heaven' a sonic boom rang out, sounding peculiarly like the blast from a tank on the summit of the neighbouring Golan Heights. The visit to the Mountain of the Transfiguration was a further Galilee highlight – taxi after taxi ferried the pilgrims to the summit of Mount Tabor, where Hope blessed them and prayed for the transforming power of God in their lives. Hope shunned the offer of a return journey in the taxi and took a half-hour walk down the 29 hairpin bends.

Ruth Gledhill decided to walk with him. It was to be one of the most meaningful walks in her life:

> I will never forget walking with him on my own. It was at a time when the Church of England was only just coming to terms with the full implications of the ordination of women and was in a real state. I was going through a bad time; personally, spiritually. From my own personal point of view I was quite opposed to women as priests and was considering my future. I was really attracted to certain elements of Roman Catholicism as well as of Judaism – which might seem odd – but there was something in both which attracted me. What happened on Mount Tabor was a heavenly moment for me. I asked David about the Rosary beads he was carrying (he carried them throughout the pilgrimage) and he explained the basics of the Rosary to me. I was fascinated, so he went on to teach me how to pray the Rosary, which I have never

forgotten. I was able to use what he taught me and it cheered my spirit. I will never forget it. Eventually, he persuaded me to stay where I was. That walk transformed me on the Mountain of the Transfiguration and I felt very close to Bishop David.

Gledhill says she was much more open-minded about the Church and its role afterwards.

The physical act of shifting over 200 people and their luggage from one place to another, on time and with precision, was a major act, but Hope relished it. The group was split over three hotels in Jerusalem to speed up the process of checking in, taking meals, and departures. Hope was based at the King's Hotel on the border between East and West Jerusalem. He had insisted on Arab coaches and drivers with Israeli guides. It was quite a mix. The BBC crew filmed Hope as he led the pilgrims from the Mount of Olives and Mount Zion to Bethlehem, where he celebrated the Eucharist in the Church of St Katherine, and to the Anglican Cathedral in Nablus Road. For the first time he wore cope and mitre in what was a splendid service. Seeing him out of his Bishop of London garb, it was brought home to me for the first time that David Hope was now Archbishop of York. But the undoubted highlight of the Jerusalem visit took place at 4am one morning as the group slept soundly. An earthquake struck. The King's Hotel was affected by a quite powerful aftershock from the quake which had its epicentre in Egypt, making the building rock. Hope tells vividly how he woke up, looked around him and felt his bed being shaken violently: 'My first thought was that it was a new system of early-morning call: actually shaking you violently to get you out of the bed. But then I realized that this was in fact an earthquake and I went to the window. It was first light and I wanted to see if other buildings had been affected. It was all over within seconds but it gave me quite a fright.'

The Times's Diary picked up the story, pointing out that Hope was sleeping on the eighth floor of the King's Hotel – and that had the building collapsed he would have ended up on top of his pilgrims, who slept below!

When Hope arrived home it was to prepare for his impending enthronement. Plans were well advanced. The Duke of York would attend. Hope had a new home to settle into and many new things to learn. It would be his third diocese in six years. London had lost a man who had given everything to bring what Chartres now describes as 'respect' back to the episcopate. 'It is a terrible blow, bad news for the Diocese of London,' said George Cassidy, Archdeacon of London and now Bishop of Southwell. The Diocese tried to be brave and acted as if it were business as usual, but Hope's departure wore heavily on morale for the remaining months of 1995. The headline in the tribute edition of *The London Link* was 'I never thought I'd say it but I am genuinely reluctant to go.'

But gone he had.

9

Ebor

Apart from the ordination of women we don't have any substantive disagreements. I like to think that one of the reasons for that is that we have both had different types of exposure to the Eastern Christian World and I think that Anglican Catholics who have different exposure to Eastern Christianity are certainly of a type.

(Rowan Williams)

To say that David Hope was concerned about a possible disruption to his Enthronement Service in York Minster by gay rights protestors would be an understatement, but in the event they spared him. By now he had had enough of Outrage!'s threats and intimidation. The new Archbishop was also understandably disorientated in those first few months in York. The after-shock of the Tatchell confrontation, the invitation to become Archbishop of York, the consequent tying-up of loose ends in London, moving house and re-establishing himself in Yorkshire, all took their toll. Hope would not admit it, even today, but he was unsettled, irritable, unsure about his next step. Quite a few people were concerned for him.

Tim Thornton, his former Chaplain in Wakefield and London, was by now principal of an ordination training course and conceded that Hope was probably tired after that year. The pilgrimage to the Holy Land had been a good thing but there was a temporary chagrin about him, totally different from his mood when he had left Wakefield for London.

The enthronement was a wonderful occasion, reflecting Hope's true spirit. A civic procession left the Mansion House just after lunch, arriving in the Minster where over 3,000 people were waiting, including the Duke of York and the Lord Chancellor. It was a bright autumn day. There was something poignant about Hope the Yorkshireman as he approached the Great West Door of the Minster. In his first address as Archbishop he spoke of the challenge of contemporary mission. The Church of England had to remember the character of previous generations as it sought to address contemporary anxiety and uncertainty about the future. Hope urged the packed Minster 'to draw upon and learn from the insights and wisdom of the past as the inspiration for the future. Past pioneers of the Christian faith had been "God bearers". They had a fearlessness, a boldness, an energy and zeal for the things of God – a missionary extravagance which was incapable of being hemmed in by the four walls of any church, committee, board or council.'

Hope also took a swipe at modern society: 'We allow ourselves too often to be satisfied with the superficial, too addicted to the quick fix, to short-termism.' What was needed was 'reflection and reflectiveness – taking the long view'. He pointed to the 'complexity and paradox of many questions which press in on our modern world, coherence of vision is to be found not in the following of a book, a theory or even a creed but in the person of Jesus Christ'. At the end of formal proceedings, Hope paused at the Great West Door and blessed the people, the City of York and the diocese.

The Diocese of York was simply delighted to have him. Hope's new flock was unaware of the toll that London had taken on him but, as he regained his equilibrium, a more relaxed and poised man emerged.

To be Archbishop of York is a strange job. You are primarily a diocesan bishop of the rather conservative and solid Diocese of York. York is much more diverse and spans a far greater geographic area than London. As a former ordinand in the diocese myself, I found that it always seemed a little too large, with many contrasting communities that do not always gel. Several of the towns – Middlesbrough, Hull, Selby and York – are worlds apart. Fortunately, a network of suffragan bishops minister to Whitby, Hull and Selby. York Minster has tried to create a diocesan-wide ministry but has had problems.

Hope, facing his new diocese for the first time, must have found the change of gear very odd after being close to the seats of government, royalty and so much of the Establishment. Westminster, Mayfair and

Chelsea had been replaced by the likes of Withernsea, Pocklington and Guisborough.

Some of his closest friends continued to insist for some time after he had left London that Hope had made a mistake. To move from number three to number two in the hierarchy was 'hardly worth it' according to one. Hope had been 'much needed and would be missed in London'. York was too provincial, not challenging enough. They thought he had gone into a retirement cul-de-sac and that London would suffer, despite the appointment of Richard Chartres. But the Northern Province did not see it like this.

Habgood had been solid, intellectual and reliable, but also detached and remote. Hope brought a reputation for warmth with him, and the diocese would enjoy it. Those in his new diocese were optimistic that he would bring vision and management skills to the Gospel in the north. One constituency – those who remained opposed to the ordination of women and who had been disappointed with Hope's position – did not know what to think. His very appointment was confirmation that the Church of England would not ignore those who shared Hope's views, but he was going to have to face some tough decisions in the run-up to the millennium.

His first Remembrance Day in the north is a good example of how different the jobs in London and York are. As Bishop of London he had led the Royal Family, government and nation in the 11am Act of Remembrance at the Cenotaph in Whitehall. The ceremony was broadcast live to a worldwide television audience. His first Remembrance Day as Archbishop was at the parish church of St Mary's in the North Yorkshire village of Old Malton. No one, perhaps, noticed this stark contrast.

Hope was soon in tune with his new diocese, however, picking up on local concerns and issues and addressing them. Education soon topped the bill. He told a congregation of education administrators, teachers, parents and children at a dedicated service in York Minster that education had become one of the most important issues affecting society. Hope always puts a good deal of work into drafting sermons and speeches with a specialist theme and he consulted widely about this particular address. He called for a partnership of interest regardless of political party or any other kind of dogma: 'Backed by noises from industrialists about the lack of self-discipline, initiative and determination to hold down any job [the current situation] really does raise the spectre of a substantial number of young people emerging as potentially unemployable simply because they have been denied some very basic educational skills.' He advocated 'the pursuit of the best and highest possible standards for all children in Britain's schools', and said that a clear spiritual and moral dimension should give each pupil guidance 'about values, qualities, standards in school, at home, in our dealings with one another as neighbours [and] in the country at large'.

He reminded the congregation of the biblical view of a person as a combination of body, mind and spirit. Each individual was to be nurtured and encouraged.

Official confirmation that the Duke and Duchess of York were to be divorced came in the spring. The announcement was expected, but the effect on the city of York was noticeable. The media were interested in Hope's view of the current state of play within the Royal Family. There were increasing marital problems for the Prince and Princess of Wales, and the York announcement only reinforced the notion of a Royal Family in crisis. The Archbishop had met the Duke just a few months earlier when he attended his enthronement. He had this to say in public: 'I am aware that such decisions are never easily made or without careful consideration. The people of York will, I am sure, wish to join me in assuring the family of our continuing concern and affection.'

Hope's first Easter as Archbishop of York was also memorable. Hope met as many people as he could. He was in Hull for Maundy Thursday at St Alban's Church, before spending Good Friday in a public procession of witness from Clifford's Tower to York Minster. He preached in York Minster on Easter Day.

Hope had great pride in the Minster, something that St Paul's had never evoked in him. Late at night, returning to Bishopthorpe after a meeting, dinner or service somewhere in the diocese, the sight of the Minster would lift his spirits: 'Look at it! Beautiful. The Minster really is an exceptional, wonderful place. Splendid. Look at it!'

In June 1996 the Irish President Mary Robinson, who was on a tour of Britain as part of the quest for peace in Northern Ireland, attended a special service at the Minster, along with the Duke of York. In his sermon, the Archbishop quoted one of the people he had come to admire in public life – the Chief Rabbi, Jonathan Sachs. Sachs' wisdom encouraged him in much the same way as Cardinal Hume's did. The view of the Chief Rabbi was that dialogue has been one of the great religious achievements of the past half-century: 'It has promoted a new mood of mutual understanding and respect. But the work has hardly begun. Religion is still used to defend ethnic or national rivalry and it still claims human sacrifices.'

On the Irish question, the Archbishop linked St Patrick with St Paulinus, urging everyone on in the quest for peace: 'In that age when Ireland was the envy of Europe for its culture, its learning and its sanctity, St Patrick wrote of his beloved Ireland, "I have made you a light for the nations, so that you may be a means of salvation to the end of the earth". And like Paulinus [the first Bishop of York] . . . of whom it was written – "he went straight on in his calling to glorify God and edify others"'.

The 31 August 1997 brought devastating news. Diana, Princess of Wales, was killed in a car crash near the Pont D'Alma in Paris. The death of an important person prompts the activation of an emergency response procedure involving senior church leaders. News organizations from across the world wanted interviews, and bishops (let alone archbishops) were in keen demand to comment on issues such as bereavement, the effect on Diana's sons, and even the future of the monarchy within the Established Church structure. Hope was woken by his private telephone line very early on the morning of the accident. Along with just about everyone else, he was still not sure whether Diana was dead or alive at that point, but was warned that she was unlikely to live. Claire Forbes, in my absence on holiday with my mother in Madrid, rang Hope at 5am and they drafted a tribute:

I was numbed when I was informed early this morning of the death in such tragic circumstances of Diana, Princess of Wales, and Mr Dodi Al Fayed and those travelling with them. Princess Diana was a uniquely attractive person whose death will be greatly mourned by very many people. My abiding memory of her will be the warmth of her personality, her vibrancy of life and her hugely compassionate heart, particularly towards homeless young people, those suffering from HIV/AIDS and more recently the victims of landmines. In commending her now into God's gracious keeping, I urge that all of us in remembering her with much thanksgiving will keep her two sons and members of her family concerned in our prayers at this time for their comfort and consolation.

Hope had met the Princess on several occasions and was genuinely sympathetic to her plight. He liked her, and was sad at what had happened to the royal marriage. As Bishop of London, he had developed strong links with royalty and he felt privileged to be close to the family in a certain, limited way. It is also clear that the synergy between Queen Elizabeth II and the Archbishop of York was positive. Hope always lit up when he talked about her and obviously enjoyed her company. It is a tradition that, when a diocesan bishop is appointed, the candidate is obliged 'to kiss hands' with Her Majesty in the same way that a new ambassador has to, as her Majesty's representative. This was something Hope did before each of his three senior appointments, but he has special reason to remember the time he kissed hands as the new Archbishop of York, because the Queen handed him a Knighthood 'completely out of the blue'.

The way Hope tells the story encapsulates a sense of surprise and disbelief:

I assumed it was a normal homage ceremony. You arrive. You put on convocation robes, the episcopal garb. Then the Clerk to the Closet stands on your right with a Bible – the Home Secretary is on your left. You line up, the door opens, and there is the Queen. She walks up to you and says good morning – or whatever – and you walk over to the Fald Stool and you kneel down – Her Majesty standing behind it – and you put your hands together and she puts her hands over yours. And you make the oath which the Home Secretary dictates to you line by line. Then you get up and the others move away and you are left with Her Majesty, who has a little word with you.

But on this occasion, Sir Robert Fellowes, then the Queen's Private Secretary, said to me, 'Well you know the form' and I said 'Yes I think I can remember.' And Willie Booth was also there, as sub-dean of the Chapels Royal, and it was at that moment that he

said 'Oh well, you will be getting a K of course today.' And then
Robert Fellowes confirmed it, in a very laid-back way. I asked him
what he meant by a K. 'Well, Her Majesty will award you a knighthood this morning.'

Just as he said it, and absolutely without any warning whatsoever, the doors opened and in we went. And it was the nearest
thing you could have in that situation to a complete surprise. After
everyone had gone, almost as an afterthought, the Queen said to
me: 'It gives me great pleasure to award you this knighthood for
the work you have done in the Diocese of London.' And she
handed it to me. I was really quite taken aback.

Hope laughs: 'I didn't quite recognize what had happened. I left, put
everything in my bag and got on the train for York, sitting there in
Standard Class with my knighthood in this kind of sports bag and
waiting for the trolley to come along so I could buy a whisky. I could
hardly believe it.'

Hope had a genuine awareness of the pressures on the Queen and
her family as Diana's body lay in a Parisian hospital. The extent to
which Britain (and particularly the media) responded to Diana's death
in part appalled him. Death, for Hope, is an inevitable part of life. To
the Catholic in him, the hysteria, the national outpouring of grief, the
return of the Queen from Scotland, the hundreds of thousands of
pounds spent on flowers, and the sense of foreboding and drama, were
over the top. He appealed for restraint and for concern for Princes
William and Harry. He led prayers for the Princess in York Minster
and a special Daily Service on BBC Radio. He had no part to play in
the funeral even though he was invited.

The death of Diana and the consequent outpouring of affection for
the Royal Family revealed, for Hope, something about the spirit of
Britain.

I think the affection in which HM the Queen is held is enormous
– you could see that when she came to York for the 2000 celebration service – people respect her, respond to her as monarch and
sovereign. She has been an icon of probity and a beacon for many
through much of the twentieth century and people will remember
her, above all, for that. Politics, in contrast, have deteriorated in

Britain – as they have elsewhere. People have lost confidence in political parties.

This convinced him of the vital importance of the monarchy as an institution, though he recognized that it would need to change and adapt.

What we need is a slimmed-down Royal Family which resonates with the people more. The fact that the Sovereign is anointed in what is a religious ceremony when he or she takes the throne is something we have lost sight of. This is a calling with God's involvement, and in stark contrast to a republic. I certainly would not want a republic. Just look around the world [the sexual shenanigans of President Clinton were dominating the headlines] and see how so many republics have resulted in the abuse, overuse, usurping of a power which is not anointed, God-given. Of course we need democracy. Of course we need politics, but the monarchy as a divinely inspired institution is both biblical and sensible and something which I warm to.

And, in a way, as we see the United Kingdom devolve we also see that a Sovereign is more important in a devolved Kingdom than in what we had before. Ultimately it is all about the unity of the people. We should hold together the unity of the nation.

The Church of England's role as the Established Church in all of this obviously has implications. When Prince Charles succeeds to the throne he will become not only monarch but will be anointed and be the Supreme Governor of the Church of England, as is his mother. The Church will move towards disestablishment but I would hope that an element of our contacts with the State will remain.

The death of Diana was pretty scary really. It was the moment when we came closest to revolution on the streets. I believe we should have learnt a great deal from what happened that day.

As he had in London, Hope made it his aim to visit each of the deaneries in his first year. The Howden deanery visit was typical. He began the day with a service in Howden Minster, a beautiful church which sits proudly in the flat countryside just off the M62 motorway near Goole. He went on to visit a farm, and Wolds Prison, and met young offenders at the adjacent HMP Everthorpe. The next stop was an encounter with managers and workers at British Aerospace. After a brief break, the Archbishop attended an open evening – an opportunity for local congregations to ask anything they wanted. This relaxed approach, which comes naturally to Hope, was in clear contrast to the more cerebral Habgood.

Such visits continued apace. They helped Hope become increasingly aware, after his years in London, of the tough task facing rural communities throughout Britain, not least in the Diocese of York. He also learned of the plight of Yorkshire fishermen. In Whitby they told him how their livelihood had been hit hard by EU fishing restrictions.

Hope had inherited John Habgood's Chaplain, David Willborne, who is a gifted communicator, humorous writer and novelist. He saw Hope established in the job before taking up an appointment the Archbishop found for him in a lovely parish in the Yorkshire Moors. Hope was then able to make his own appointment.

Mike Kavanagh is a trained psychologist and there were a few jokes about his former job when his appointment was announced. He reflects: 'It was brave appointing a psychologist as his Chaplain. The Archbishop often used to joke about the fact that I watched his body language to see what mood he was in. His permission to tell it straight was important. I have always been able to tell him things that I thought he ought to hear. More often than not this might be me simply telling him that he needed to take some time out – away from it all.'

The election of a Labour Government after 18 years of Conservative rule was the highlight of the second year of his time as Archbishop. Hope was cautious about the prospect of a Labour victory, but stressed the need for everyone in the country to be more positive. A Leader in *The Times* on 11 January was astonishingly supportive: 'Hope is an effective theological college principal and skilful Bishop of London who shows every sign of proving an impressive Archbishop of York. Offering a gentle, and welcome, reproof to earlier interventions from other bishops interpreted as supportive by Labour, Dr Hope argues that "overriding pessimism has to be tempered and balanced by a recognition of some positive factors about where Britain is".'

Hope had argued that the Church and government should be more positive about Britain and its place in the world order: 'The Archbishop', continued *The Times*, 'also displays a more sophisticated approach to tackling want than many of his colleagues . . . there is evidence from across the world that welfare destroys as much as it protects.'

The election campaign was already under way, amid a public clamour for change, on Easter Day. Hope spoke boldly from the pulpit of York Minster: 'As members and participants in this new order we all have a particular and immediate responsibility as we approach the forthcoming General Election. There are just over four weeks yet to go. Does this Easter Day have anything to say to us about our approach to the election and the issues which are before us? Not in a narrow political sense, but in a way which must surely challenge every party and its politics.'

This, said Hope, is what the new order of the resurrection was really all about. The key concerns, he went on, needed to be with 'developing a longer-term vision for human flourishing' and 'consolidating and fortifying national confidence rather than the pursuit of short-term expediencies'.

Hope needed to make some difficult and controversial decisions in the Diocese of York. He adopted the role of chief executive when it came to budgets and personnel, focusing on the key words 'priorities' and 'resources', but his pastoral touch was always present. Mary Murray, who had been PA to Habgood, gave an interview to *The Times* about working with her new boss and revealed what Hope was like as the man in charge:

My role has changed [since Hope arrived]. Before I was PA to Dr Habgood and worked with Mrs Habgood in the palace. Then David Hope came and he had no wife so I am now palace manager and head of 16 staff, which is a hoot. I'm also PA, so I have three roles. This is his home, his base, this is his security from a human point of view, and he relies on me to keep the whole thing ticking over. My hours are nine to five with a bit added on. He has early-morning prayers, he's up at 5am, opens his mail and has done a day's work by the time we get in.

Murray has run a tight ship which Hope has appreciated and valued – as long as boundaries between his official office and his limited free time have been respected and observed.

The General Election campaign coincided with two visits by Hope to other dioceses – Newcastle and Liverpool. They gave him a snapshot of some of the issues facing the Church of England. In Newcastle, under the guidance of Alec Graham, who was about to retire as Bishop, I saw at first hand how people responded to the new Archbishop – with enthusiasm mixed with a plea for encouragement to help them make the Church grow. The Catholic clergy were particularly demoralized in some inner-city areas. Since the ordination of women they felt rejected and undervalued.

Hope also visited the Diocese of Liverpool and preached in Liverpool Cathedral where he had been ordained exactly 30 years before. 'I can tell you it was quite something going into that pulpit and thinking, my goodness me, I have come here as Archbishop of York.' The new Archbishop toured Warrington and Wigan, having lunch at HMP Walton before seeing the Edge Hill district.

New Labour and Tony Blair swept to power. Remnants of Thatcherism disappeared overnight as John Major was defeated and Tony Blair arrived on the doorstep of No. 10 on 2 May. Hope liked and respected Major (this was before his affair with Edwina Currie came to light), but there was undoubtedly a sense of the party having been in power for too long. After 18 years, the Tories were torn apart over the question of Britain's future in Europe and their reputation was badly tarnished by several cases of corruption which would later result in the imprisonment of Jonathan Aitken and Jeffrey Archer, and in Neil Hamilton – accused of asking questions in the Commons in return for cash – losing his seat to Martin Bell, a white-suited anti-sleaze candidate.

Overseas trips were very much on the agenda in 1997. Hope returned to Romania with the European Children's Trust in June and established important contacts, visited projects, met government representatives and enjoyed a level of hospitality which once again endeared him to the people. In September, Hope attended the Golden Jubilee of the Church of South India. The Church has 2.8 million baptized members, over 10,000 congregations and 2,200 pastors divided into 21 dioceses. ✠David Ebor was appalled at the levels of poverty which he found in some parts of the country. Nor did he mince his words when it came to the spiritual poverty of God's creation: 'There is a spiritual crisis in almost every part of the world, a spiritual bankruptcy – a longing and hunger for the deep things of the spirit.' There was a clear statement that the political process was limited: 'We are not to be conformed to the dull mediocrity of this world, but to be transformed.'

He began to dread the frequent journeys to London as Archbishop. Every week there was one, if not two, journeys south for committees or meetings. He always travelled Standard Class and, in the early days after privatization, Hope was infuriated with the service offered by the Great North Eastern Railway franchise holder, writing to the chairman frequently about the lack of punctuality and information, poor air conditioning (which caused breathlessness at times) and in-adequate refreshment facilities. Christmas, on a different note, saw Hope co-presenting the BBC1 Christmas morning show with Fern Britten. The programme was recorded at the Castle Museum in York and featured various pop stars and personalities.

By 1998, Hope's diary had settled down, but it was still ridiculously demanding. There was a Royal Schools of Music Festival in York Minster that October which he attended a week before joining the people of Ripon for a festival walk in honour of St Wilfrid, their local saint. During the year, Hope also opened a social action centre in Scarborough, installed new canons at York Minster, joined the Sisters at Horbury Convent, Wakefield for their 140th anniversary, and attended the farewell gathering for his archdeacon of the East Riding. He travelled to Finland for ecumenical discussions, and said goodbye to James Jones who left Hull to be Bishop of Liverpool. It was frenetic.

Rowan Williams, as a Bishop and then Archbishop of the Church in Wales, remembers David as a highly effective and astute Arch-bishop. From across the Welsh border, Hope was seen as Catholic and welcoming – cutting across the perceived 'Forget that lot in Wales' view which was too often displayed by some bishops. 'I think it's true to say that some people in the Church of England were not terribly aware of the existence of the Church in Wales and I suppose there was always the feeling that when the Welsh bishops met the Church of England bishops it was very much a case of the tenants meeting the landlord. But not so with David.' Williams remembers his inclusiveness, his warmth and concern for the Church in Wales, or indeed for the Church anywhere: 'When he came to preach at David Thomas's Consecration [as Provincial Assistant Bishop of the St David's Diocese in Wales] it was such a positive sermon – it echoed the experience of the Church there and helped a lot. I always remember thinking just how helpful David had been.'

It is probably rare for the Church of England to have two such complementary Archbishops of Canterbury and York. Williams and Hope are warm, friendly and affable. They radiate honesty, integrity, a love of the Church and a passion for the Gospel. They are Catholic and inclusive, divided on only one issue. The Archbishop of Canterbury says: 'Apart from the ordination of women we don't have any substantive disagreements. I like to think that one of the reasons for that is that we have both had different types of exposure to the Eastern Christian world and I think that Anglican Catholics who have different exposure to Eastern Christianity are certainly of a type.'

Hope's theme that Christmas was 'A Nation at Ease with Itself' and there is some suggestion that he rather enjoyed this quasi-political swipe at some of society's ills. He focused first on Romania and India and talked about the psyches of those two very different nations. Then he moved quickly to modern Britain: 'What do we say of ourselves? A country in which a new government swept to power just nine months ago with high hopes and expectations and where already some commentators are somewhat cynically posing the question: "Has anything really changed?"' But Hope did not like the idea of a nation at ease with itself anyway. He preferred the notion that a nation should, rather, have a vision of what it can and should be. 'If we are truly not only to capture but to be caught up in the vision of God then nothing less than a spiritual revolution is called for. In ourselves, our society, throughout the world; a celebration of the fact that the world is charged with the grandeur of God and that the glory of God is celebrated in each and every person fully alive.'

Hope's assessment of Tony Blair as Prime Minister is balanced and critical: 'There is a fundamental goodness and integrity about Blair. I don't think there is any doubt about that. There is an innate Christian understanding and sense about him which wants to do the decent thing. I have a clear respect for him.'

Fine words, but Hope's tone belies them: he winces, is searching for words which can sum up the sense of disappointment which he believes many people share in Blair and Labour. He finds them:

For instance, everyone was led to believe this 45-minute warning business before the 2003 Gulf War. Now I believed it and I based my theological reflection on it. I believed there were weapons of mass destruction that could be used within 45 minutes and this was a determining factor in my assessment as Archbishop about what Blair was doing. So, on the basis of what I knew, I was supporting him. In the end, it looked as if [the weapons] didn't exist and then the war became more of a worry to me.

Hope believes that the Labour Government has meddled too much in people's lives: 'The Government wants to interfere in every detail: there is an element of control-freakery about Labour, which will only be realized in the fullness of time, when the books are written.'

Hope was invited to preach in Turku Cathedral, Finland, offering thanksgiving for progress that had been made between the Scandinavian churches and the Anglican Church. Choosing to focus on the life of the English martyr Henry, after whom Turku Cathedral is dedicated, and Bishop Thomas – Bishop of the See in 1229 – Hope used the past to give confidence in the future. His conclusion was that debate, schism, misunderstanding and disunity had always been a part of church life and yet everywhere, in people's lives and faith, there were examples of truth, tolerance and love. These were the true signs of hope: 'There is, yes, comfort and encouragement; there is also exhortation and judgement. We cannot escape the controversy and the conflict which inevitably God's word brings upon us – ourselves, the Church, the world.' Pointing to Ephrem the Syrian, Hope reminded his international congregation that Lent was a time to go back to basics – fasting, reading the scriptures, celebrating the sacraments.

As the first anniversary of the death of the Princess of Wales approached, Hope had had enough of the endless analysis, brooding and infatuation, and felt strongly enough to speak publicly about the inability of some of the media to 'let Diana rest in peace'. He gave an interview which was splashed on the front page of the *Sunday Times*

(5 July 1998) and headlined: 'Archbishop urges end to "Cult of Diana"'. It is only with hindsight that one can see how successful Hope's intervention was. He said:

> We need to begin to move on and part of that moving on is the letting go. It is hard to do this with a constant stream of photographs of her every day. We need to be aware of clinging to the icon. There is some element of wallowing in her death. After all, the memories are so vivid. Let's not get totally swept up in indulging our emotions but instead reflect on her life and ask, 'What does this mean for me?' From my own pastoral experience, we do need to let go of the person and to embrace more of the positive things that we remember.
>
> If people have a particular memory of Diana they should honour this by getting in touch with the charities she championed. Her compassion and her care are the things we should be reflecting on as a society, not just indulging our emotions.

Christopher Morgan is convinced that this was one of the most effective and timely ecclesiastical and episcopal interventions: 'Overnight, Hope changed the mood. The media did let go. The amount of coverage subsided significantly and even the build-up to the first anniversary of her death on 31 August was subdued.'

Hope also made a triumphant return to his former London parish when he preached at All Saints, Margaret Street on All Saints Day. Here was an opportunity to call for Catholic revival and renewal: 'Our forebears in the Catholic movement were zealous for the transformation of the Church and the conversion of England. That task remains and if we are to address ourselves to it we need not only to recover the full meaning of Catholic – in the sense of wholeness and inclusiveness – rather than to be issue-driven and exclusive.'

Hope urged his former congregation to seek out God's vision and not to follow their own: it was a rallying call. Hope was in vintage form.

> We desperately need to recover this vision of the Church which is God's and not ours; where yes, we recognize readily the brokenness and sinfulness of our frail humanity – knowing our need of God –

yet, at the same time, rejoicing in the abundant mercy and grace of the God who in Christ has come among us and alongside us; who accepts us just as we are, and whose Holy Spirit is already at work in and through each one of us in this sacramental celebration for transformation and change, the dust of all feebleness, frailty and sinfulness, into the gold of his glory.

Somehow, the *Sunday Times* managed to interpret this emphatic celebration of the Anglo-Catholic tradition as a personal attack on George Carey. An advance copy of the text had resulted in the headline 'Archbishop in shock attack on Carey' but the substance of any 'attack' was so insignificant as to be non-existent and no other media took up the story.

Also in 1998, Hope first met Alan Hydes – a local portrait painter and TV personality. It is rare for Hope to be inspired and impressed by someone so quickly as he was by Hydes. The idea was that Hope would sit and chat with Hydes while his portrait was painted. Not only was the programme an interesting one, but the resultant portrait still hangs in Bishopthorpe. Many visitors believe that it is more representative of Hope's character than the official one in the drawing room which I referred to at the beginning of this book.

He also agreed to become an occasional member of the BBC Radio 4 *Daily Service* presenter's rota. This involved writing a 15-minute script, travelling to Didsbury, Manchester to the church studio early on the day of broadcast for two hours of rehearsals followed by a live broadcast. Hope was not bothered by any of this, even though it is unusual for an archbishop to be on such a general rota – they are usually called in do special occasions – and enjoyed the experience.

Just before Christmas, US and UK allied forces again went to the brink of serious hostilities against Saddam Hussein in Iraq. Britain found itself isolated from her EU neighbours and was accused of being a puppet of the United States. Hope agreed to a joint statement with the Archbishop of Canterbury urging restraint but supporting hostilities if the rule of law continued to be flouted. Privately Hope thought it was outrageous that the West had been dragged to the brink of such action once again.

These early years of Hope's time as Archbishop of York were form-ative for the rest of the episcopal ministry. Full of activity, with the emphasis on meeting people and getting out and about, Hope under-pinned everything with a daily cycle of prayer, meditation and reflection. He enjoyed his annual trip to the Isle of Skye and the occa-sional opportunity to meet with friends and relax, but the vast majority of his life was taken up with ministry and service. He became one of the more experienced bishops in the House of Bishops. He was, overall, more relaxed and in control of his own destiny (under God) than he had ever been since his consecration in York Minster as Bishop before his move to Wakefield.

Hope had made a quick impression on bishops and clergy in the Northern Province. They appreciated his humanity and integrity. John Packer, who became Bishop of Ripon and Leeds in the early years of Hope's time at Bishopthorpe, regards Hope as hugely encouraging: 'I have always found David is extremely supportive in my own ministry and I frequently turn to him for advice. He is among the most unpretentious people I know and yet has a quiet dignity. This means in particular that his worship is accessible and human. Barbara [Packer's wife] and I well remember his kindness when we spent the night at Bishopthorpe before my ordination as Bishop in 1996.'

As the millennium approached, Hope was to face some new and very demanding issues both from a theological and sociological standpoint, but his experience and confidence were both on the increase. He had certainly regained not only his balance after the London years but a new peace and sense of contentment which many had not seen before.

10

Millennium

Only those in the centre can have a view of the whole. They cannot run it and should be too few in number to be tempted but they can nudge, influence and if they have to, interfere. The centre's principal task is to be the trustee of the future, but it needs to be sure that the present does not run out before the future arrives.

(Charles Handy, *The Empty Raincoat*)

The marking of the Millennium was widely perceived as a national disappointment in Britain. David Hope saw celebrations at the Millennium Dome in London's Docklands as a massive anticlimax. It was a politically correct mishmash in which the birthday of Jesus was subsumed. The enduring image on 31 December 1999 was of the reigning monarch, the Supreme Governor of the Church of England, singing with crossed hands in what looked like an aircraft hangar. The Dome was a monument to poor government and a missed opportunity. Hope felt sorry for the Queen. In the regions and in local communities, celebrations were more of a success. On Christmas Day 2000, Hope told a packed congregation in York Minster: 'The millennial year has witnessed here in York, and in the region more widely, a number of remarkable events and celebrations. Who can forget the scene towards midnight at the dawning of the new Millennium when the great West Doors of this Minster were opened to witness huge crowds both within and without?'

But, that Dome? Hope's northern blood told him that huge amounts of money should not have been spent on such a monstrous white elephant. Dominic Lawson, Editor of the *Sunday Telegraph*, was particularly attracted to Hope's view and, over the year, made frequent references to those 'who, like the Archbishop of York, have questioned the wisdom of the Dome project'. The Archbishop wrote an article for the *Sunday Telegraph*, contrasting the Dome of St Paul's in the City to the Dome in the east:

> The paradox . . . is well demonstrated by those two domes: on one side of the Thames, the Greenwich Dome, recently constructed at huge cost and in which human achievement is celebrated by the display of the very latest advances and the glorification of the icons of the future. On the other side, Paul's dome, undoubtedly built at great cost in its day, but for all that, constructed to the glory of God and, in the name of Jesus Christ, significantly surmounted by the cross.

With George Carey unapologetically peddling the government line, there was a rare display of archiepiscopal disagreement as the Archbishop of Canterbury told *The Times*: 'The designers have caught very much the importance of Christianity at the heart of the Millennium celebrations. Other faiths are not excluded by any means, but people will see the significance of the Christian faith.' The Archbishop of York was unimpressed and refused to condone or countenance the Dome. Even Labour stalwarts such as Chancellor Gordon Brown privately admitted reservations.

Hope used his passport frequently as the twentieth century came to an end. Trips to Finland, Romania, the Middle East and New York were all on the agenda in 1999. During the previous year, he had undertaken a highly successful visit to Australia where he had visited the Dioceses of Adelaide and Willochra and it is clear that the prospect of travelling was more appealing to him than it had been in previous years. In Finland he attended the consecration of Dr Jukka Paarma in Turku Cathedral in January 1999.

By far the most important event in Hope's life in the last year of the century was the purchase of a beautiful cottage on the banks of the River Ribble in the Yorkshire Dales, nestling on the edge of a small market town. Hope discovered the joys of making his own home for the first time. Since the death of his parents, he had had full access to the bungalow they lived in next door to his sister and her husband in Wakefield, but it was not his own home in the way that his cottage would be. The cottage was remote and comfortable, at night enveloped in a profound silence. When he visited, there was plenty of time to walk and meditate.

Also reflecting his increasing confidence in his work and ministry, he resolved never to take any work to the cottage; it was to be a place purely for relaxation. His only problem was the lack of opportunities to get away. There were some signs that his health was beginning to suffer as a result of the punishing archiepiscopal schedule. The reoccurrence of back problems, muscular aches and pains were symptoms of hard work and stress: 'I suppose it is my body saying to me that you cannot keep up the relentless timetable of events, travelling, etc. without respecting the need for relaxation and reflection.' Whenever he could, he set off for the cottage, lit a log fire and cooked simple meals.

Hope focused on the search for peace in Northern Ireland and the Middle East in his 1999 Easter Day address. He told his York Minster congregation that Easter stressed

> The respect and dignity which is owed to every human person, quite irrespective of ethnic background, race, colour or religion . . . Politicians, negotiators, envoys, mediators, diplomats and their advisers must seek as frequently as they can to explore possible points of contact, to open up new avenues of mediation in the hope that sooner or later opposing factions will return to the negotiating table with serious intent towards a genuine and just resolution.

After Easter, Hope visited the Diocese of Bradford. He had faced multi-faith issues when he was Bishop of Wakefield rather than when he was Bishop of London. After a civic reception at the City Hall in Bradford, Hope saw how inter-faith chaplaincy worked in local hospitals. The following day, he saw the contrast of the Craven archdeaconry where he experienced rural ministry in the same diocese.

The death of Cardinal Basil Hume, Cardinal Archbishop of Westminster, in June 1999 was a personal blow. The two men had been good friends during David's time in London. Hume's body lay in state in Westminster Cathedral prior to his funeral. Hope offered a Requiem for the Cardinal, but decided not to travel for the actual service. In a moving tribute, he summed up his respect and sense of gratitude for Hume's ministry: 'I always enjoyed my meetings or telephone calls with him. Despite the seriousness of the task before us, he would often find time to chat about more general and personal matters. After the vote on the ordination of women in the Church of England, he would occasionally telephone to keep in touch and to ensure that friendships as well as the more formal relationships between the two churches continued to be nurtured.'

His diary reflected a different pace and variety. He joined the people of Oldham to celebrate 150 years of Oldham Borough Council before acknowledging the 40th anniversary at Scargill House, a pioneering Christian community and retreat near Kettlewell in the Yorkshire Dales. Hope had to replace Gordon Bates, Bishop of Whitby, who retired in 1999. Bates had supported Hope with great enthusiasm, despite having served under John Habgood for many years. He was replaced by the Archdeacon of Lancaster, Robert Ladds. At the same time, Hope promoted the Vicar of Boston Spa, Richard Seed, to succeed the ubiquitous George Austin as Archdeacon of York. Hope also consecrated George Cassidy as Bishop of Southwell, Nottinghamshire, in York Minster. This was a personal pleasure, for Cassidy had been Archdeacon of London under Hope and the two had worked well together, but he had been less happy in London after Hope's departure. Southwell inherited an able and competent evangelical priest who had battled in London for many years even before Hope's arrival. Hope visited the Diocese of Southwell on Thursday 8 July when he was honoured with an Honorary Doctorate of Divinity at Nottingham University.

Mike Kavanagh, Hope's Chaplain during these years, saw the relationship as one of friendship as well as of archbishop and priest:

Our working day would start with a chat in his office. It was when I could tell how things were with him. Often, we had time to comment on the beauty of the river and the early morning light marking the changing seasons. The view from his office must be one of the best in the Church of England. But sometimes it was a brief hello and a sense that he was preoccupied with the burden of work – sermons to write, visits to prepare, pastoral problems to sort out. At such times he would withdraw a little, and the playfulness that he so often showed over coffee was not there. At such times, all of us in our own way prayed harder for him knowing that we could only do so much to lighten the load.

He never forgot the staff who worked for him – he often knew their families and the issues they were facing and he was interested in their well-being without traversing a personal boundary. All the staff appreciated the small but significant ways in which he cared for us. Fan heaters would be turned on in the office on cold winter mornings, windows opened in the summer. There were always notes of appreciation and words of thanks at the annual Christmas lunch. He was not demonstrative but he was a warm and kind person at work; when he said 'How are you?' it really was as if he cared how you were.

Romania was once again on the agenda as the last few months of the twentieth century ticked by. The Archbishop visited the Christian Children's Fund projects in Cluj in the summer, after the seemingly unending days of the General Synod Meeting in York. Hope's brief to look after communications became especially demanding as it was realized that the abolition of the Church of England's communications committee had not been such a bright idea: there was now no qualified body to monitor the Church's image and performance in the media, which came to be seen as a great oversight. Hope also spent some time with young people from all over the Diocese of York for a weekend at Wydale Hall near Scarborough. Hope enjoys the company of young people but somehow remains very much the Archbishop in their presence. He ate with them, went on a long walk and enjoyed the weekend away. Steven Croft, Warden of Cranmer Hall, the Durham theological college, spoke at a similar meeting at Bishopthorpe Palace a few weeks later for all those preparing for ordination in the Church of England.

Hope's relaxed confidence in his own judgement when pressure mounts was also manifested when it was revealed that one of his recently appointed suffragan bishops was having matrimonial difficulties. Richard Frith, who had taken over as Bishop of Hull from James Jones, promoted to Liverpool, discovered that his wife was having an affair with a priest in the south west. David, as Archbishop, tried to help but it became more and more obvious that Mrs Frith had left the bishop's house and that the story would break. When the media did find out, Hope issued a statement of support for his Bishop, urging prayers for the family and all concerned. He was genuinely concerned for Richard as well as the people and churches of Hull, but he was strong and resolute in his belief that good would prevail. Richard has remained grateful to Hope for his solid support and Hope is full of admiration for Frith's ministry.

It was interesting to observe Hope's reaction at first hand when he visited New York for the first time in November 1999. He found the cut and thrust, even after London, surprising and disconcerting. I guided the Archbishop along 43rd Street in the direction of Times Square and will not forget the expression on his face when he saw the cacophony of neon lights and noise. 'What a place!' he exclaimed with a mixture of laughter and disbelief. The Parish of St Thomas's Fifth Avenue had invited him and he spent the whole of the Sunday preaching and speaking. Once again, Hope took the forthcoming Millennium as his theme, urging that the focus be on the Christian dimension, avoiding 'individualism and self-centredness and self-gratification'.

'We need to seize the opportunity which the Millennium gives to focus again on those norms and values which, as well as celebrating our diversity, serve to nurture our being and belonging together as friends rather than enemies, as neighbours rather than strangers,' he told them in a moving and well-received address.

Back in London, Hope spoke at a special breakfast, organized to launch some forthcoming Walsingham Regional Festivals. With him on the bill were David (now Lord) Putnam, the film director, and the late Dame Thora Hird. In a sober and rallying call for the Christian community not to forget the real message of the year 2000 he said:

The Millennium is not only about the past and the present – it is most importantly about the future – after all, that is the real point of God's coming to us in Christ. Walsingham sets before us the glory of God in the face of Jesus Christ. The challenge before us all is whether we shall learn the lessons of the past so that we may be better people in the future. More importantly, like Mary, as Christians all of us are called with greater generosity and self-sacrifice to respond more readily and eagerly with our 'Yes' to God – for him, and in him, for others.

The Millennium seemed to dominate every aspect of the media, but the Archbishop of York was increasingly sick of it. Hope made clear and concise plans for his own Millennium celebrations, agreeing to take part in a special service in York Minster on New Year's Eve, spending the rest of the time between Christmas and the New Year at his Dales retreat.

Thirteen months after January 2000, Hope provided a vivid insight into how he saw the English Church responding to a fast-changing, secular culture in Britain. In a revealing lecture ('Changing Church: Unchanging God') given in Cambridge in February 2001 he gave a summary of where he thought the Church had got to. Models of the Church in the twenty-first century depend, for Hope, on the under-standing of Church as the New Testament describes it ('true vine', 'bride of Christ', 'spiritual house', 'household of God', 'fullness of Christ', 'servant') but from that starting point, realism and conviction is required: 'The Church's vocation then is to live and witness as a fellowship, a communion, a *koinonia*, which seeks to be one in its ecclesial being, and one in its will to serve its Lord: and in mutual love which gives individuals and local communities and diverse Christian traditions scope fully to be themselves and to participate equally in the common life.'

Hope described the Church as a kind of interactive vehicle of God in a society which had lost its path, that had veered off the road. God is Father, Son and Holy Spirit – the essential Trinitarian mystery – and yet the Church's ability to represent God and to be his presence was under threat. And, until priorities were sorted out, Hope would continue to use this kind of language, which the Cambridge audience seemed to respond to.

To conceive of the Church as a pilgrim people must raise questions for us about the nature of our structures. Of course, for any group or organization, institutional arrangements are inevitable and necessary. The difficulty and the danger arises when these very institutional arrangements become ends in themselves; when they dictate the nature, shape and function of the organization. It is a warning that structures need to be kept to a minimum and that we must constantly be asking questions about what we need at the centre. To which the response can only be 'as little as possible' and only that which manifestly and absolutely cannot be done and effected more locally. In any case it might be worth asking, where is the centre?

This perfectly sums up Hope's view of the Church and how it is organized. He has been greatly influenced in his thinking by the social philosopher and management guru Charles Handy. Referring to his book *The Empty Raincoat: Making Sense of the Future*, the Archbishop quotes from the chapter on subsidiarity and the concept of the 'new centre'. 'Only those in the centre can have a view of the whole. They cannot run it and should be too few in number to be tempted but they can nudge, influence and, if they have to, interfere. The centre's principal task is to be the trustee of the future, but it needs to be sure that the present does not run out before the future arrives.'

Hope always sees the big picture and can pinpoint global weakness. To this extent he is an example of a corporate chief executive who recognizes that other people have to make decisions but that they need feedback, encouragement and guidance. In many respects, Hope's calls for a freer and more Trinitarian Church became clarion calls, but they were rarely acted upon. The Church regarded him as a Yorkshireman speaking common sense, but did not save his words in the prophetic file. So Hope, in that Cambridge lecture, simply reminded the Church that unless it assumes a prophetic mantle and looks outwards rather than dissipates its energies inwardly, it will fail to communicate the Good News message entrusted to it:

The centre properly understood must be multi-polar – that is at once the myriad manifestations of the One Holy Catholic and Apostolic Church in every place as much as it is diocese, province, worldwide communion . . . New models and new patterns both of being Church and of mission and ministry are emerging both in the urban and rural areas . . . Here at the heart of it all is a call to holiness, a holiness which is our humanness, each of us made in the image and likeness of God and the Church a place of sanctification and transformation.

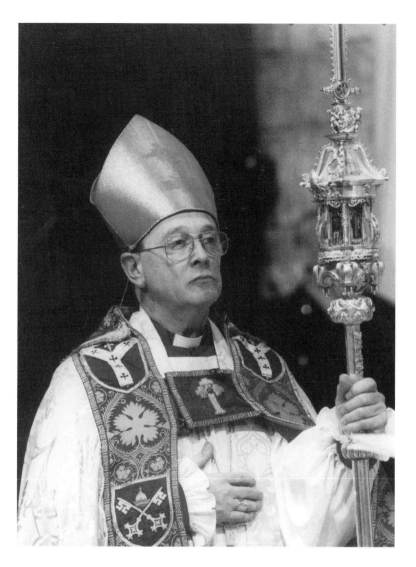

11. Dr David Hope moments before his enthronement as
Archbishop of York in 1995.

(Evening Press York)

12. (From left to right) Archbishop of Canterbury, Dr George Carey, Archbishop of York, David Hope, Bishop of London, Richard Chartres, and Alan Chesters, then Bishop of Blackburn, at a ceremony to mark the unveiling of Hope's portrait as Archbishop of York. (July 1998)

13. Hope pictured with Her Majesty the Queen, at the inauguration of the newly elected General Synod of the Church of England at Church House, Westminster. (November 2000)
(Bishopthorpe Palace Picture Library)

14. Pope John Paul II invited Hope, along with other Christian leaders, to Rome in 2000.

(Servizio Fotografico de 'L'O.R', Vatican)

15. Hope as Inspecting Officer taking the Royal Salute to celebrate the Anniversary of the Coronation of Her Majesty the Queen, at Museum Gardens in the City of York. (June 2001)

(Evening Press York)

16. Gay Rights activist Peter Tatchell outside York Minster where he planned to attach this poster to one of the doors, outing the Archbishop. (July 2003)

(PA Photos)

17. Hope watches the rising floodwaters
outside Bishopthorpe Palace. (November 2000)
(PA Photos)

18. Hope beside a footpath that runs alongside his Bishopthorpe Palace.
The footpath was closed due to the foot-and-mouth crisis. (March 2001)
(PA Photos)

19. Hope with the Archbishop of Canterbury, Dr Rowan Williams, at Church House, Westminster. (July 2004)

(NI Syndication/Benn Gurr)

11

Floody Hell

The traditionalists clapped ecstatically as Dr Hope blessed them, papal fashion, as he processed out at the end of the two-and-a-half hour Mass. These traditionalists, whatever Dr Carey and the rest of the Church of England may think, are not going to go away.

(Michael Brown)

Paradoxically, it is the floods of 2000 for which Hope will be best remembered around York. Towns and villages along the River Ouse endured some of the worst floods in living memory. The Archbishop's palace was affected and he set about raising community spirit by donning his wellington boots and spending several weeks visiting devastated areas.

For recession-hit farmers and a country already suffering from rail chaos and fuel-price protests, and now widespread flooding, 2000 certainly was a year to remember. In November, Hope had decided to spend a few days at his Dales cottage and noticed that the weather forecast was far from promising. Severe fronts brought torrential rain to high ground, with rivers and streams filling up at an extraordinary rate. Hope's cottage was close to the River Ribble and a weir, and he was aware of the ferocity of the water. As it transpired, there was no danger to the cottage, but as parts of York city centre succumbed to the Ouse, with homes, shops and hotels flooded, it became clear that Bishopthorpe was increasingly vulnerable. When Hope arrived back at the palace on a bleak evening the Ouse had already encroached on the rear of the palace, covering the terrace and gardens. Any further serious rainfall and the whole building would be affected.

For many in low-lying areas, this was the second time they had been flooded out in a matter of months. They could only watch helplessly as the waters rose again, ruining newly replaced carpets, decorations and plasterwork. Eventually, Bishopthorpe was almost cut off. Travel was difficult if not impossible and the A64 near York and the A19 at Fulford were closed because they became impassable. This left just two major roads in and out of York, and very long traffic queues. Rail services, already suffering from maintenance and safety problems, were thrown into chaos, along with bus services. It seemed as though nowhere in North Yorkshire was unaffected by the disaster. The police, fire, ambulance service and army helped evacuate stranded families from their homes by boat. Filling and distributing sandbags by toiling around the clock was the only way to attempt to hold back the water. The severity of the flooding was underlined when the Prime Minister flew in for a lightning visit to see the scale of the disaster. This was tokenism at its worst. Hope met him, but was not at all reassured or impressed by what he saw as an act of opportunism.

By now, muddy water was seeping up through the stone floors at Bishopthorpe Palace, and staff moved the more valuable objects to safety. The Archbishop's wine cellars looked seriously under threat: 'I'll have to keep an eye on the wine –look at it! look at it!' Feelings of frustration and helplessness increased around York. At one point the electricity was cut off at the palace as water reached power circuits, and Hope had to move into an adjoining flat. 'It was quite atrocious and after visiting people as far apart as Selby in the east and the more northern parts of the Yorkshire Moors I really couldn't believe how terrible it was. People's lives, their livelihoods, their family life were ruined for weeks.' Keith Massey, a freelance cameraman, asked the Archbishop if he would be filmed surveying the floods for overseas television footage. Hope trusted Massey and agreed, if Keith would show him even more of the worst-affected areas.

The consequence of CNN beaming pictures around the world of an archbishop flooded out of his ancient palace was that people immediately started sending in donations for renovation work. The press office was inundated with calls: 'How can we help?', 'What can we do?' The congregation of St Thomas's in New York's Fifth Avenue, where he had preached the previous year, sent $10,000.

The pictures of Hope in his wellington boots, struggling around the towns and villages trying to make contact with devastated people, were memorable. He arrived at the Royal Oak Pub in Old Malton which bore a sign saying 'Still open – and no, we haven't watered the beer down' even though the pub could only be approached by boat, or those wearing anglers' waders. Juliet Stimson, the landlady, was living upstairs away from the water with her three children.

Hope also witnessed a tractor 'taxi' service in Norton, with farmers ferrying residents from their homes to dry land. He said: 'I think it was fantastic that, amid scenes of such devastation, desperation and despoliation, people were displaying the sort of humour they were.' As he left the pub he noticed someone had put a lifebelt near the pub door and written TITANIC on it in felt-tip pen. Hope remembered the words of Psalm 69, 'Save me, O God! For the waters have come up to my neck . . . I have come into deep waters, and the flood sweeps over me.' *The Sun* carried a large picture of the Archbishop looking Noah-like with the caption 'Unholy Water . . . Archbishop of York Dr David Hope at flooded HQ'. The paper proclaimed that this was 'Drench Warfare!'

One of the most hilarious stories of the floods came out of the Archbishop's need for a haircut. Hope asked Mary Murray to check with Nick the local hairdresser to see if he had managed to open his business. His shop was at a higher point in the village. Nick said that there was floodwater around the salon but Dr Hope was free to go for his monthly trim. Hope put on his boots and waterproofs and left the palace on foot, and arrived to find a war-like spirit. Three women were at various stages of having their hair set or permed. They greeted David, and he sat in the waiting area while Nick rushed from one customer to the next and the phone rang incessantly. One woman was wearing the bottom part of a rubber diving suit – something Hope found it difficult not to comment on. Then, right in the middle of a complicated procedure involving a client's hair, the phone rang again. Hope could see that the harassed Nick was unable to answer, so he grabbed it himself: 'Good morning, Nick's Hair Salon, how can I help you?' said the Archbishop. Nick looked on, open-mouthed, and whispered to his other customers how Mildred would never believe that it was the Archbishop of York who had changed her hair appointment from Wednesday to Monday because she was flooded out!

Hope began to feel more at home at Bishopthorpe, even though it was hard for him to find privacy. He began to enjoy the routine of staff arriving for a day's work followed by an interminable round of receptions, meetings, launches and visits which stretched into the evenings and weekends. One of the most public areas at the palace is the river terrace, because of the regular flow of boats on the Ouse, many of which turn around alongside the palace. Jack Nicholls, Bishop of Sheffield, remembers a dinner Hope held for his episcopal cell – all bishops belong to a cell of half a dozen of their fellows, which meets regularly to offer mutual support. Nicholls says:

At the time we met at Bishopthorpe the cell included the then Archbishop of Canterbury, George Carey; the Bishop of Lincoln, Robert Hardy; the Bishop of Oxford, Richard Harries; the Bishop of Southwark, Tom Butler and myself – plus wives. We were having supper on a warm summer evening on the terrace overlooking the river. It was a jolly party after a few glasses of wine and a delicious meal. Very informal; shorts and T-shirts were the order of the day. All was peaceful until we were interrupted by a large riverboat filled with tourists which proceeded to turn round immediately in front of us and from which emerged the dulcet tones of none other than Archbishop David Hope. 'Welcome to Bishopthorpe, the home of the Archbishops of York' we heard him say in a little pre-recorded speech. We cheered and raised our glasses to the said Archbishop, and pointed to him, indicating him to be the voice on the tape. Amused as they were, I doubt that the passengers realized who the rest of the company were and I doubt that they would have believed it had they been told.

Hope was 60 in 2000. He spent his birthday at a church leaders' consultation and did not mark the great day, but he was pleased to get his Senior Citizen's travel card. After a period of niggling medical complaints ('more minor things than anything major') he was again in rude health.

There was no better way for Hope to mark 2000 than with a return pilgrimage to the Holy Land. Because he had made such a journey before, this trip was more relaxed than that in 1995. He left London in early March – a few days before the group of some 280 pilgrims, who came from all over the country but particularly from the Dioceses of York, London and Wakefield.

The pilgrimage was organized by his chaplain, Michael Kavanagh, and a team from the diocese. The venues were the same: Galilee and Jerusalem. 'I want people to have time to reflect on where they are going, what they are seeing, on the element of pilgrimage and faith which establishes so much of what they have only previously read or dreamt about.' His sister joined the pilgrimage. It was Anne's first trip to the Middle East, and her presence added to Hope's enjoyment of the tour. He soon resumed his tour-guide's banter of 1995, and his ability to communicate one-to-one with so many people meant the pilgrims felt it an enormous privilege to be in the Holy Land with Hope in the millennial year.

One concern of those organizing the pilgrimage had been the later decision of the Vatican to organize a papal visit to the same area. Thankfully, Pope John Paul II arrived the day the Archbishop left Israel. As the Archbishop followed the life and ministry of Jesus around the holy places, it was clear that the Pope would receive a very special welcome. Numerous Vatican flags flew alongside those of Israel and Palestine in the places the Pope would visit.

Hope began his pilgrimage with a meditation on the Sea of Galilee, then celebrated the Eucharist at the Mount of Beatitudes. During the course of the week he did the same in Jerusalem, Bethlehem and Latrun and led a renewal of baptismal vows on the shores of the River Jordan. As the week went on, the pressures evaporated. Hope relaxed, enjoyed the fellowship and friendship of his very own congregation and took part in a colourful evening at a Palestinian restaurant in Bethlehem. Having offered thanks to the guides, drivers and spiritual leaders, Hope lead the pilgrims in the conga around the hall. It was quite a sight.

The pilgrimage was a good preparation for Holy Week. As Archbishop, Hope always started Holy Week at Parcevall Hall, the retreat house of the Diocese of Bradford, owned by the Shrine of Our Lady of Walsingham. The millennial year also brought with it an invitation from HM The Queen and The Duke of Edinburgh to attend one of the Royal Family's more relaxed dinner parties, and to stay the night at Windsor Castle. The Queen and Duke showed guests around the restored castle.

Two former Archbishops of Canterbury died within a few months of each other in 2000. Donald Coggan, one of Hope's predecessors as Archbishop of York, died peacefully on 18 May. Coggan had also gone on to be Archbishop of Canterbury, and Hope paid tribute to the work of the well-known evangelical preacher and teacher: 'He is remembered throughout the Diocese of York and more widely in the Northern Province with much affection, where in his 13 years as Archbishop his distinguished biblical scholarship, his devoted pastoral care of clergy and his deep love of people were always so clearly evident.' Robert Runcie's death in the summer of 2000 provoked more analysis and debate. Humphrey Carpenter's biography of Runcie some three years earlier, in which Runcie was indiscrete about establishment figures from the Royal Family down, had been serialized in *The Times*, and he was roundly criticized for his indiscretions.

In a conversation I had with Runcie 18 months before his death, he was generous in his assessment of Hope's ministry: 'He is remarkable really. I am so pleased he succeeded John Habgood and has done so well. Send him my best wishes and my commiserations. Retirement is wonderful.' Hope liked Runcie, but he never really enthused about the general drift of the Church under his leadership. Nevertheless, Hope probably had more Catholic respect for the liberal Runcie than for the evangelical Carey.

Hope's tribute at the time of his death was heartfelt: 'Robert Runcie was a dedicated priest and Bishop and served the nation as Archbishop of Canterbury through some difficult and unpredictable years in the 1980s. He will be remembered for his sharp intellect, colourful personality and wonderful sense of humour – which never deserted him even in more recent months when he was obviously suffering greatly.'

Just a few months after both David and the Pope were in the Holy Land, the Archbishop had an opportunity of an audience with His Holiness. Pope John Paul II invited his Grace to Rome with other Christian leaders from the north of England after Easter. He was joined by the Roman Catholic Bishop of Middlesbrough, Rt Revd John Crowley and the Methodist Revd Stewart Burgess, who organized the visit. The Pope, a very frail and yet still-alert presence, grasped Hope's hand and held on to it for several minutes. Hope will not forget that clasp of hands. He felt supported and supporting.

The importance to David Hope of Walsingham – to which he turned his attention immediately after the trip to Rome – is very strong indeed. In the company of its people, Hope lightens and relaxes. 'We should keep Walsingham as it is: no change for the sake of it – no messing about: Walsingham is where we pray for Mary to intercede for us and it is wonderful. That Holy House is a very special place!'

Hope had agreed to inaugurate a series of Regional Festivals in York Minster on the day that he returned from Rome. The highlight of the festivals was that the Image of Our Lady would actually 'attend' the event, brought specially from Walsingham for the occasion. Hope knew that he was among friends at such events but had not attended a National Pilgrimage at Walsingham for several years. In 2000 he did, celebrating the Millennium with vigour and joy. It is no exaggeration to say that, as he processed through the streets with thousands of pilgrims, this priest and Bishop remained a central hope for the future for many in that crowd.

But there was an even bigger Anglican Catholic event just around the corner. A 'Christ Our Future' celebration at the London Arena in the city's Docklands – an impressive auditorium which seats 10,000 people – was a massive show of force by English Anglican Catholics. The stadium was full. Hope was the chief celebrant while the Bishop of London, Richard Chartres, preached the sermon. Michael Brown, writing in the *Yorkshire Post*, captured Hope in a colourful review of the event: 'The traditionalists clapped ecstatically as Dr Hope blessed them, papal fashion, as he processed out at the end of the two-and-a-half-hour Mass. These traditionalists, whatever Dr Carey and the rest of the Church of England may think, are not going to go away.'

Hope's official portrait as Archbishop – with which we started this book – was unveiled at Bishopthorpe Palace at a party on the Sunday lunchtime during the July sessions of the General Synod in 2000. It was a hot and balmy Sunday and among the great and the good were the Archbishop of Canterbury and the Bishops of Blackburn and London. The portrait was commissioned by the Corporation of Church House and was painted by Andrew Festing. Interestingly, despite my daily conversations with Dr Hope, the Archbishop made no reference to the painting until the day the portrait was unveiled. The portrait is a deep and penetrative study of Hope's more serious side. He is wearing convocation robes (rather than cope with mitre in hand) and his whole demeanour is stoical and serious. Staff at the palace do not recognize their Archbishop in the painting because of the absence of a smile, or even a twinkle in the eye. Hope will be remembered at Bishopthorpe as a 'very funny' and 'down to earth' Archbishop while his portrait, which hangs in the drawing room along with likenesses of all the archbishops of the twentieth century, is 'serious', 'grave' and 'authoritative'.

Hope received a Millennium Honorary Fellowship from Liverpool John Moores University, having been chosen by the retiring Vice Chancellor, Peter Toyne. Liverpool had not forgotten that the Archbishop of York had begun his public ministry on Merseyside. The visit of Queen Elizabeth II and the Duke of Edinburgh that summer – at his personal invitation – was another one of the highlights of 2000 for Hope. He described the York Minster service as a celebration of life and faith in the north. Each of the 14 dioceses in the Northern Province had been invited. Over 30 bishops also attended. Hope took the opportunity in his sermon to pay tribute to the 'saints of the north who are depicted beneath the Primatial Cross of York'.

The first Bishop of York, Paulinus, 'was a missionary prepared to take risks – to leave the comfort and the safety of his own home, his own place, his own country and in obedience to the Lord's command to go and preach the Gospel, to make disciples of all the nations. [He] found himself in an alien culture and among a hostile and pagan crowd.' And Hope did not forget the vision of St Hilda of Whitby: 'Her presence among the array of northern saints bears testimony to the contribution which women have made not only to the life of the Church but the life of our communities more widely, to the towns and villages of northern England. Women not only in the home but in the workplace, women of enterprise and skill, women of perseverance, courage and heroism.'

Hope, with the Queen listening intently, turned his attention to the plight of Britain's countryside: 'The rural areas and the farming communities need and deserve our strongest support at this time. For their communities, like the shipbuilders, the weavers of wool and the spinners of cotton before them, are now in crisis.' Hope had, by now, visited all 14 dioceses in the Northern Province as Archbishop of York.

The Archbishop had come to know his flock, and of their needs and concerns. During 2000, many of those he ministered to had been touched by calamities, and had gained comfort from him. Before the year was out, there was to be another disaster. On 17 October, the 12.10pm GNER service was dramatically derailed 17 miles into its journey from London Kings Cross to Leeds. The train, carrying about 200 passengers at 115 mph, left the tracks as it approached a sweeping bend. The buffet car, in the middle of the train, took the full force of the derailment, broke away from the rest of the carriages and flipped on to its side. Four were killed in the buffet; 35 other passengers were injured. The front six carriages hurtled along the track for a further 100 metres. Many of those caught up in the tragedy were from Hope's diocese and province, and once again he did what he could to minister to the injured, and to the bereaved.

The year 2000 had been a time in which Hope's very practical brand of ministry had been of immense comfort to many people. Away from the disasters, it was also a year of personal happiness and great fulfilment. Hope was at his best, enjoying every minute of his work in his sixtieth year, and aware that there was still a great deal to be done.

12

Calamity in New York

Terrorism has become a feature of our modern world . . . that corrosive evil of resentment and hatred and revenge, deeply embedded within the human heart and mind and which becomes the motivating and driving force of the zealot and the fanatic.

(David Hope, York Minster)

David Hope was growing in confidence and enjoying his work as a Bishop more than he had ever done. *Common Worship* – the new Church of England Prayer Book – was published. His attendance at the newly elected General Synod at Church House, Westminster, in November 2000 saw him in fine form. His sense of humour – a wonderfully wicked ability to see the funny side of things – was stronger than ever.

A dinner engagement on the eve of Synod saw a friend of Hope suggesting they meet in Trafalgar Square to find a suitable restaurant in which to discuss Synod business. Hope asked: 'Where on earth will I find you in Trafalgar Square?' The friend suggested meeting outside the Whitehall Theatre. Hope struggled in driving rain down Whitehall and sought refuge under the theatre awning. He had been standing there for about five minutes wearing his purple shirt and clerical collar when he decided to see what play was on. His faced drained in horror: the show was *Puppetry of the Penis* and the theatre was plastered with posters and publicity pictures. Hope beat a quick retreat to the sanctuary of a bookshop doorway and made his views more than felt when his colleague arrived. 'Having me standing in that doorway with all those pictures of penises with faces. Honestly!'

Some in the Catholic wing of the Church of England felt frustrated by what they regarded as Hope's 'too quiet' leadership, but he was resolute in his belief that, as the number of women candidates for ordination rose dramatically and the nature of the Church of England changed, a period of calm was crucial. One critic says: 'We started to realize that Hope never had been and never would be a party man. Some of the more vehement Catholics failed to understand his views, while others regarded him as a cool and committed leader. In many ways, Hope is seen as a paradox: intensely private and distant, yet also warm, gentle and vulnerable. I suppose many of us who want to know him better find him elusive.'

One of the younger clergy in the Diocese of York was upbeat when asked for his perception of his Archbishop.

He is bloody down to earth. If ever you have a problem you know that he will listen and be both firm and fair. I am impressed by him, like him, and find him to be a very human person. He is warm and positive and held in high regard by all traditions among the clergy. Many of the laity remark that this is a holy man. John Habgood was more remote and we needed the warmth of a man like David Hope here in Yorkshire. This is a difficult and disparate diocese covering a wide geographical area with an intense collection of urban and rural issues. David Hope has presence and the people love him; we are very lucky indeed.

A new rail crash shocked everyone in late February, 2001. Just after 6.10am near the village of Great Heck, between Goole and Selby, a Land Rover towing a car on a trailer driven by Gary Hart drifted off the M62, ran down an embankment and on to the tracks of the East Coast main line. Hart scrambled to safety and was still on the phone to the emergency services when the 4.45am GNER train from Newcastle to London King's Cross hit the vehicles at around 125mph. The collision derailed the passenger train, throwing it into the path of an oncoming goods train. Six passengers and four rail employees died and 76 people were injured. Hope had intended to be on the train himself, but changed his plans at the last minute.

The dead, the injured and the emergency services involved were all from his diocese and province. Chaplains (many of them from the

Diocese of Sheffield) did a remarkable job offering bereavement counselling. Hope kept in touch with what was going on. He would later visit the crash site and lead a memorial service and service of thanksgiving at York Minster.

During the service he said:

> The cascade of totally unforeseen and unexpected circumstances on that morning demonstrates to us the fragility and frailty of our life in this world, which is in fact with each one of us every day of our lives . . . St Paul speaks of what he describes as 'the groaning and travailing of the whole creation' and certainly over recent months – first the floods, the rail accidents, now the foot and mouth crisis – all these things conspire to oppress us with those altogether more profound and ultimate questions about our world. They certainly make us stop and think.
>
> Yes, there was the tangled wreckage that Friday morning which I still remember so vividly. But there was also on the horizon the first signs of the dawn of a new day – the sky shot with the beams of the morning sun. There, in that moment, yes, the destruction and the desolation of one day, the new possibilities, the new life of another.

Hope spent a weekend in Rome during Lent 2001 with another group of pilgrims. It was the first time he had led a pilgrimage to Rome and prayers were said for peace in the Middle East. 'Today, here in the place where the Apostle Paul suffered martyrdom for the sake of Christ, it is very appropriate that we should be attending in particular to this part of his Letter to the Ephesians. For here is a letter sent to all the churches of the East, reminding them of the supreme task of the Church – that of being Christ's instrument for the universal reconciliation of human persons one with another.'

Hope reinvented 'Agenda for Action', his key mission strategy in the Diocese of London, as 'Living the Gospel' for the Diocese of York. He again urged all branches of the Church to produce a Mission Action Plan (MAP) which would help focus their work and mission: 'If we were able to activate and effect all these plans, the Church throughout the diocese would be immeasurably strengthened.' The response from the parishes was upbeat and many saw

'Living the Gospel' as his key missionary activity as Archbishop of York.

Of all the issues Hope had to contend with as a Bishop, the devastating foot and mouth outbreak of 2001 was one of the most profoundly difficult. The disease was terrible for many of the communities in his diocese and province.

You could sense the desperation and helplessness. Communities were under siege. The country's image abroad was that of a land of burning animal carcasses, suicidal farmers, cordoned-off countryside and a Ministry of Agriculture which simply failed to keep up with events.

Hope had the courage, after visiting several areas where whole herds had been destroyed to prevent the spread of the disease, to call on Tony Blair to abandon any plans for a General Election while foot and mouth was on the rampage. But his call came about almost by accident and, bizarrely, involved Dame Thora Hird, the actress.

Hope was in London for a meeting of the directors of Walsingham, who had to cancel the annual May Bank Holiday pilgrimage because of the outbreak. After attending that meeting he went on to take tea with Dame Thora, who was approaching her 90th birthday. She and the Archbishop had been friends for over a decade and they chatted in front of a photographer for *The Times* newspaper, the Archbishop asking her questions about her life and career. Ruth Gledhill was present. The photographer wanted a close-up of the Archbishop and the actress, and Thora asked: 'Excuse me. It doesn't look as if we have just come out of the bedroom does it?'

Ruth had probably sensed that her afternoon might be worth more than a picture story, and asked a serious question: 'Have you come across many of the effects of the foot and mouth crisis in the diocese, Archbishop?'

'Oh yes, certainly,' Hope replied.

'Do you think they could call a General Election with things as they are at the moment?' It was widely believed that the government planned to call a General Election on 3 May, although this was never announced.

'No, I don't think people in the countryside could stomach it.'

Thora sipped her tea. Ruth's journalistic antennae rose. 'Have you said that publicly Archbishop? I mean, would you?'

Hope went off to St Matthew's, Westminster, where he had organized a reception for all national religious affairs correspondents. Since leaving London, Hope had had less call for such informal, bridge-building events. During January and February 2001, however, relationships between the religious affairs correspondents and the Church of England communications department had sunk to a new low, and Hope was concerned. The *Guardian*, the *Daily Telegraph*, *The Times*, *Church Times*, the *Sunday Times* and the *Sunday Telegraph* all showed up and, over wine, pork pie and chicken satay, the Archbishop sought to establish the nature of the problem. It was a positive and hearty meeting.

Chris Morgan of the *Sunday Times* took me to one side. Would the Archbishop consider a call in the paper next Sunday for the General Election to be postponed? I told Christopher that Hope had just uttered exactly those words to his colleague on *The Times*. Gledhill needed 24 hours to talk to as many other bishops as possible and *The Times* was so delighted with the story that it was splashed on the front page. Hope realized on the train back to York, 14 hours after he had left home, that he had lit a blue touchpaper.

That meeting with the journalists had its own impact. It brought to a head concentrated discontent among journalists that they simply did not know what was happening in the Church. Dr Bill Beaver, a friendly American who had succeeded Eric Shegog as Director of Communications, had found the going tough. An able operator, Bill would be on his way to a new post within a matter of months. It seemed that the Communication Director's post was an almost impossible one, and it would be frozen for 18 months. Peter Crumpler replaced Beaver early in 2004 as Communications Director.

From the moment *The Times* hit the streets at 10pm that night, all hell was let loose. International and national news agencies, BBC *Newsnight*, the *Today* programme and every other newspaper and agency wanted to dig into the election story. The Archbishop was the 'shepherd of his sheep'. Hundreds of thousands of cattle, sheep and lambs were being slaughtered and buried. The countryside in Britain was in crisis. Blair had to listen to Hope. The next morning Hope appeared at a press conference at Bishopthorpe. His was the strongest, clearest voice so far expressing the level of despair in the countryside. Hope gave numerous interviews and was in sparkling form. The paradox was that Hope felt genuine sympathy for the plight of Prime Minister Blair. The foot and mouth crisis had so obviously botched the government's plans for a 3 May election and, as the Prime Minister had taken personal control of the handling of the crisis from his beleaguered Minister of State for Agriculture, Nick Brown, he toured the country looking forlorn and concerned. Hope recognized this.

The Conservative leader, William Hague, also called for the election to be postponed between Hope speaking to Gledhill and the interview being published. It looked as if the Archbishop had come in on the back of Hague, but this was not the case. Stephen Bates (*Guardian*) had a radical exegesis to offer:

> Dr Hope's concerns for the plight of the farmers in his diocese and across the whole of England is genuine. They, and he, have had a rough winter. The last time the Archbishop made national waves was when he was pictured in his wellington boots trying to salvage his wine cellar from the autumn floods lapping up to his thirteenth-century official residence . . . His remarks certainly dragged the Archbishop of Canterbury, George Carey, in their wake. Dr Carey yesterday issued a statement emphasizing that it was not for the Church to dictate the timing of the election. There is a debate among bishops about the desirability of an election. Yesterday the bishops of Oxford, Durham and Salisbury – all with rural dioceses – suggested that it should go ahead as soon as possible.

This may be a good moment to focus on the politics of David Hope. It is true to say that he has not always found it easy to convert his Christian convictions into a cross on a ballot paper. He is, instinctively, a small 'c' conservative, carrying in his genes a northern, no-nonsense self-reliance tempered with a Christian compassion for those who struggle to make it in life. He had no empathy for the aggressive self-reliance espoused by Margaret Thatcher, but a good deal more time for the more socially inclusive policies of John Major. Tony Blair, and New Labour, connected with him emotionally, because they had adopted many of the sensible, inclusive policies that had traditionally been espoused by one-nation Conservatives, but intellectually he doubted their sincerity.

Easter 2001 could not come soon enough. It was a late one and Hope was tired. The floods, rail chaos, petrol shortages and now the foot and mouth outbreak made this a lambing season to forget. But the joy of the resurrection was proclaimed as ever in his York Minster Easter sermon. It was Hope against adversity:

Over recent months in the country as a whole and certainly here in the north and in North Yorkshire, people have certainly felt oppressed and downcast . . . The resurrection of Jesus is both a past event and a present reality. Today we are risen with Christ. It is also hope for the future . . . This ancient and venerable Minster has witnessed many Easters in very differing circumstances and situations, but perhaps none more so significant and straightforward than on Easter Eve in the year 627 when Paulinus baptized Edwin, King of Northumbria, and Christianity itself was reborn and flourished in these northern parts.

The election was finally held on 7 June. Labour was returned with another massive majority, which Hope had feared. 'A landslide victory for any party is not good for democracy. A real democracy needs a healthy opposition. Lord Acton's dictum that absolute power corrupts absolutely holds good today.'

His relationship with the Roman Catholic Church, even after the death of Cardinal Hume, continued to flourish. In the summer, Hope had the opportunity of preaching at Vespers at a gathering of Roman Catholic leaders in Ampleforth. During a moving and spiritually uplifting sermon, Hope took an ecumenical opportunity to pay tribute to the monastic movement. 'Such surely has ever been the monastic quest and vision – itself that sign of protest and contradiction to which the whole Church is called – in simplicity and holiness of life . . . Benedict himself makes the important point that the Christian life, however it is lived, wherever it is to be found, is a journey.'

After another summer relaxing near Settle, and his two-week hike to Scotland, Hope was refreshed and renewed. He had a new vigour and determination. Just before the world was completely and utterly turned upside down by the events of 9/11, Hope undertook a trip down to the Diocese of Portsmouth where he delivered a lecture enabling him to spell out once again the important role of the parish church structure, as well as some of the problems that had to be faced. The day before the lecture, he delivered a sermon at St Mary's, Portsea, where he found solace in the life of the Blessed Virgin for the world and the Church: 'Times have certainly changed, greatly and radically, but mission has not and it is Mary's song, the Magnificat, which gives us some of the clues by which we might take forward the same mission entrusted to us by God into this twenty-first century. Mary's God is no churchy or religious God. Her God is the one who brought down the powerful from their thrones and lifted up the lowly.'

He urged the congregation to build the Kingdom and not the Church. Paying tribute to those who had led Catholic revivals in history, Hope celebrated the way they 'combined the worshipping of God in the beauty of holiness with being there, out and about in the local community'. He reflected with affection on the significance of the image of Our Lady at Walsingham in the Holy House: 'Mary is not anxiously holding on to her child, nor is the child clinging to its mother, rather Mary is holding the child on her knee, looking out, facing those who are looking at and facing the image and facing the child. Mary is holding Jesus out to the world. She who has borne him in her womb now offers him to the world.'

Using this understanding of mission and commitment, Hope presented a radical way forward for the Church. The audience in Portsmouth represented a wide range of church and other guests. Hope always enjoyed these opportunities to grapple in depth with issues as the politician in him emerged out of the pulpit. The message was stark: 'Our society has undergone a process of geographic, economic, social and cultural polarization.' Dismissing the constant refrain that churches were losing members and closing, Hope hit back: 'The survey of Hull churches recorded that churches are con-sistently engaging large numbers of people who are not part of their worshipping communities and that the Church represents an impor-tant part of the voluntary sector within the city.'

He also wanted to emphasize his own experience that affluence and poverty are equally evident in both rural and urban areas. 'Poverty and need do not admit of any distinction between urban and rural – the problems and the pains as well as the challenges and the possibil-ities are the same for both.' He paid glowing tribute to *Faith in the*

City and the consequent work of the Church Urban Fund, of which he was now a great supporter: 'Certainly for me as a very raw diocesan bishop, just beginning an episcopal ministry in the Diocese of Wakefield, *Faith in the City* provided the necessary stimulus and spur to a whole new way of approaching ministry and mission throughout the diocese.'

Prophetically, just 48 hours later, when the clock was ticking towards the hijacking of the first aircraft to crash into the World Trade Center, Hope stressed: 'A true community is where everyone has a place and a value. There is, of course, the debate about what is a community and the current trends towards redefining community into communities of interest, leisure and so on, as well as location.'

After all the calamities of the new Millennium, no one could have predicted the sheer horror and gravity of what was to unfold, and its worldwide consequences, on 11 September. The catastrophic attack at the heart of the United States – at the Pentagon and the destruction of the two World Trade Center towers in New York – resulted in unprecedented diplomatic and political activity and the inevitable retribution by 'the West' against terrorists in Afghanistan. Hope was pensive, and gravely concerned by the unfolding events. I personally had him dragged out of a meeting at Bishopthorpe Palace to tell him of the aircraft hitting the various targets. His response was to fear where such an attack was to take the world, but he was also aware of the immediate effect on relations between good Muslims and good Christians in Britain.

On the day after the tragedy, Hope said: 'We watched the clouds of dense black smoke rise from Manhattan Island and it began to resemble something akin to a doomsday scenario – Armageddon in our very midst. We are with the people of the United States of America in our shock, our profound grief and in our distress – old York at one with New York.'

The following Saturday he arranged an impromptu memorial service at York Minster and was slightly perplexed at the lack of publicity this very Yorkshire tribute to the victims received. 'Terrorism has become a feature of our modern world . . . that corrosive evil of resentment and hatred and revenge, deeply embedded within the human heart and mind and which becomes the motivating and driving force of the zealot and the fanatic . . . It should make us all think very seriously indeed about those qualities and values which are needed if a civilized world and society is to survive into the future.'

While the war rhetoric was gaining momentum, the Transport Secretary, Stephen Byers, announced that Railtrack – the organization responsible for the railway infrastructure in Britain since denationalization – would go into liquidation. Shareholders would lose money. In the same week it emerged that one of Byers' aids had released a memo on 11 September urging government spin doctors to 'bury' news while the eyes of the media were elsewhere. A month after 11 September, when it was confirmed that Ms Jo Moore had sent out such a memo, Dr Hope agreed it would be no bad thing for the government to hold an inquiry into the affair and to look at the management of news during pastorally sensitive times.

The Archbishop's intervention provoked a vicious retaliation from Downing Street. On 21 October the *Sunday Express* had the story that the government had decided, after the Archbishop's 'attacks' on the government over the railways, flooding, foot and mouth, the timing of the election and now the poisonous spin machine, that any reform of the Upper House would ensure that Hope was not offered a life peerage on his retirement.

But the tenor of the story was extremely pro-Hope and anti-Blair. Indeed, Downing Street had misjudged media respect for Hope. The headline was 'Has he [Blair] no shame?' The story read: 'Downing Street's attack on Hope comes amid an avalanche of criticism about Labour's obsession with spin . . . the Government source let it be known that Downing Street thinks Dr Hope, who was appointed by John Major and frequently met with William Hague, is a closet Tory.' The paper's leader column could not have been more supportive: 'New Labour's penchant for spin has sunk to disgraceful new levels in recent weeks and last night it got worse . . . Clearly the Government would rather the Archbishop kept his mouth shut instead of standing up for what he believes in.'

Hope did not respond. Such a story, exclusive to one newspaper, always produces a frenzy from its rivals, determined to catch up. The rest of the media got behind the Archbishop and used the whispering campaign to beat the government. The *Yorkshire Post* was typical in its response the following morning: 'If a Christian prime minister cannot accept criticism from the leaders of his own faith, how can it be said that this is a war for freedom and democracy?'

Downing Street rapidly backtracked on the subject of Hope's punishment. Such claims, it was said by a prime ministerial spokesman, were absurd. But, in private briefings to journalists – several of whom contacted me – Downing Street was not dismissing the story.

George Carey enjoyed better relations with the Blair government than with the Major administration. He rejects the view that Blair was against the Church or its hierarchy: 'This Government listens to the Church. We have opportunities to present our case and we are listened to.'

As this grim and calamitous year drew to a close, Hope was, as usual, dreading Christmas (he despairs of the commercial trappings which obscure the meaning of the occasion for so many), but he urged everyone to look at God's light in a world of darkness. His Christmas Day message was clear: 'This is the task for all – in government, in our communities, in the media, in our churches, in our schools, in our homes, an engaging with each other in that communality which brings light and life to all, thus overcoming the darkness of separation and division.'

He told a gathering of lawyers at Holy Trinity Hull just a few days before Christmas: 'The God who in the beginning made light to shine out of darkness which covered the face of the whole earth, in the birth of his only begotten Son, Jesus Christ, has intervened finally and decisively for the whole family of humankind, in the entire created order.'

13

Succession

David was the only person who bothered to contact me during that time. He acknowledged that this would be a problem for Jane and myself and the two children and it helped me more than I can say. I really did have no idea what was going on. It was David's initiative to call. I immediately got a real sense of trust and support. And throughout that whole year, from the speculation to the appointment and the enthronement, David was consistently supportive.

(Rowan Williams)

Ever since he was Bishop of London, Hope had been privy to what must happen in the event of the death of the Queen Mother. When that sad day came, on 30 March 2002, Hope was honoured to be asked to read a lesson at the funeral in Westminster Abbey, which followed a period of national mourning and thanksgiving for her life. The procession of her coffin, on the Friday after her death – at the great age of 101 – from the Queen's Chapel, St James's Palace, to Westminster Hall for the lying in state, was a memorable day. Hundreds of thousands of people visited Westminster Hall, with queues snaking back for miles at times.

Hope paid the following tribute:

Her Majesty, the Queen Mother, has had a unique place in the affections of people, not only in this country, but throughout the world. Her devotion to duty and her steadfastness in the face of adversity was an immense support and a beacon of hope to many,

133

particularly during and after the Second World War. Personally, I remember her as someone of great faith, of sharp mind, an amazing memory for detail, immense dedication to her country, with a keen interest in others and always with a sparkling and cheerful humour which endeared her so readily to so many people.

Hope also officiated at a memorial service in York Minster, which the Duke of York attended. 'There can be no doubting whatsoever the Queen Mother's sense of dedication and service,' Hope told the congregation.

The funeral was George Carey's last major state occasion. He rose to it well. His address at Westminster Abbey was one of his best, catching the mood even of the tabloid newspapers. The Archbishop of Canterbury told mourners she embodied 'strength, dignity and laughter'. Carey said: 'Like the sun, she bathed us in her warm glow.' The royal death coincided with the Golden Jubilee celebrations of Her Majesty the Queen. There was a national outpouring of love and affection for Queen Elizabeth, partly spurred on by sympathy that she had lost both her sister, Princess Margaret, and her mother, in the space of just six weeks.

The numbers of people who turned out to greet the Queen and Prince Philip as they toured Britain on her Golden Jubilee tour was truly remarkable. The final parade down Pall Mall with a fly-past by Concorde surpassed all expectations. Hope held a service in York Minster on Sunday 2 June and paid tribute to the Queen. The memories of his childhood came flooding back: his family, gathered around the 10-inch black and white TV set, watching the young Princess take on the massive responsibility which had now been hers for half a century. 'Her Majesty has fulfilled the promises made at her Coronation through a life of unstinting service, profound wisdom and courage and a clear, unswerving Christian faith,' he said. Hope also paid tribute to the extraordinary amount of voluntary work done by the Royal Family, hitting out at sceptics and critics alike:

Those altogether more depressing prognostications by the cynics among the commentators, writers and broadcasters have been considerably confounded by the absolutely natural and entirely spontaneous enthusiasm for the Queen in the year of her Golden

Jubilee and which we see overwhelmingly demonstrated this weekend throughout the entire nation.

After a hectic time, Hope led his first pilgrimage to Turkey in the footsteps of the early apostles. But this time, instead of spending most of the time in a coach or a hotel, the pilgrimage was mainly on board a flotilla of luxury yachts – each of which took around 15 people. The group visited Ephesus and other key sites around the southern coast of Turkey. Hope quickly adapted to life on board: 'It was wonderful really. The day was a mixture of several hours sailing, a visit to an historic site, worship, eating, drinking and fellowship.' The group, over 80 of them, really enjoyed the experience and Hope reckons it was one of the best trips he had been on. He agreed to take another, two years later, in 2004.

It was the election of the new Archbishop of Canterbury which dominated the religious agenda in 2002. George Carey was, at last, on his way and the race was on to succeed him. Despite the fact that only six per cent of the population go to church on Sundays, and the Church of England had diminished influence in national life generally, the interest in the choice of the next successor to St Augustine was significant. As in the previous races leading up to the appointments of Carey, Runcie, Coggan and Ramsey, bookmakers opened betting on the race to Lambeth and the newspapers produced copy pinpointing the current form of several Prelates.

Rowan Williams, Archbishop of Wales and a figure of massive theological clout, was clear favourite from start to finish. But there had to be at least a few contenders from the Church of England before a Welshman could be elected to lead the Anglican Church in England. Richard Chartres, Bishop of London, was an early starter, ruled out as the race went on because of his views on the ordination of women. He was not helped, of course, by the fact that Hope was at York. A surprisingly strong candidate throughout (and possibly because Carey had come from behind the leading pack to win the race before) was the Bishop of St Albans, Christopher Herbert, a fine chairman, teacher and a relatively unknown, exciting prospect. Radicals favoured Michael Nazir Ali, Bishop of Rochester, as a candidate whose advancement would say a great deal about the modern Church of England, and about multicultural Britain. The safe-pair-of-hands candidate was the Bishop of Winchester, Michael Scott-Joynt, a happy, capable and prayerful Bishop who would have coped well with the pressure of the office.

And then, at just 62, there was David Michael Hope. In so many other eras and contexts there is absolutely no doubt that Hope would have been an automatic choice to succeed Carey. But this was not the time or the place. First, Hope did not want the job. Second, he had made up his mind that, having been a Bishop for almost 20 years, he wanted *less* pressure, not more. Third, with more and more women in training for the full-time ministry and being appointed to senior positions, his views on women priests reflected a minority view. Finally, as was soon to become clear, there was unfinished business on the gay issue, something which Hope simply would not have wanted to deal with.

The process of appointing a new Archbishop of Canterbury centres on the Crown Appointments Commission, a mixture of bishops, clergy and laity who deliberate together before producing two names which are sent to the prime minister. Confidentiality is obviously required by all of those involved. The names of those who sat on the commission which selected Rowan Williams are now well known, and included David Hope. The Chair was Dame Elizabeth Bulter-Schloss and, along with Hope, the members were Viscountess Brentford, Archdeacon Judith Rose, Professor Anthony Thistleton, Caroline Spencer, the Bishop of Dover, Ian Garden, Revd Hugh Broad, Brian McHenry, the Bishop of Leicester, and David Kemp.

Hope's seat on the commission was a key factor in the decision-making process, and effectively ruled him out of consideration for the post. It was clear that certain candidates were discarded almost immediately and that, for most of the time, there was no doubt who the majority wanted as the new Archbishop of Canterbury. Hope refuses, even now, to confirm or deny the fact that he was in favour of Rowan Williams' appointment.

Shortly after the commission had broken up, and with two names on their way to Downing Street, Ruth Gledhill telephoned me. 'I am confident that Rowan Williams is the next Archbishop of Canterbury and I am going to splash it tomorrow,' she said. Ruth is a professional, competent journalist, sure of her sources and, that evening, she sounded convinced of her story. Not only that, her source had obviously had a direct link to the Crown Appointments Commission. Hope was livid, furious – the air was blue. But in his anger he did not blame the journalist (even though he was extremely disappointed that she chose to run the story) but demanded a full, immediate inquiry without acknowledging whether or not the story was true. 'Williams to be Next Archbishop of Canterbury' was the *The Times* headline on 20 June 2002. This was news even to the Williams family.

There was speculation that Williams was not Carey's personal choice and Lambeth immediately distanced itself from rumours and leaks, stressing that it had absolutely no comment. This put Hope in an increasingly invidious position. He spent the next day involved in a series of detailed and confidential calls to everyone involved, not least the chair of the Crown Appointments Commission, Downing Street and other bishops. 'I will find out if I can,' was his refrain. Although not quite on the same Richter Scale as the sources saga resulting in the suicide of the government weapons expert David Kelly, which led to the Hutton Inquiry, the question of a journalist being able to protect her source was the key issue involved, and Hope had to recognize this.

It was at this moment that life for the Williams family changed for ever. They had not been consulted, contacted or informed. They could not have been, for the Prime Minister had not yet had a chance to act on the recommendation. They knew absolutely nothing but were reading all this copy and were suddenly inundated. The appointment would not be confirmed for several months, and in the meantime the Church was gossiping about a prospective archbishop whose appointment had not been confirmed, who had not agreed to take up the post and who came from a clearly different ecclesiastical stable to the current incumbent. It really was a terrible mess.

Hope focused on dealing with the leak. I remember a surreal Friday evening, ten days after *The Times* story, when he asked me to meet him for supper. On my way to the palace he called to say that he had not had time to prepare any food so would I drop by at Bishopthorpe Fisheries to collect haddock and chips? He would have a glass of wine ready. When I arrived, Hope showed me into his private kitchen.

There was an air about him; he was charged, angry. 'Rob, and I mean this very seriously,' he said. 'You will find out for me who it was who told *The Times* that Rowan had been appointed. Not only that, you will find out who told Ruth all the other things which were alleged to have gone on at the Crown Appointments Commission. I am going to ask each and every member of that group to swear to me under oath that it was not them. Rowan is in an invidious position whatever the truth of the story.' The conversation continued and I felt pretty helpless. I really did not know anything more than I had when Gledhill had called me.

'But surely,' I said, 'the Church will have to either confirm or deny the story. We can't let it run for months until an official appointment.'

'How can we confirm something which has not gone through the due process – even if it was true? That is what is so terrible about the timing. I am not prepared to say anything about what did or did not happen, but ask Ruth to tell me who it was that told her these things. We simply cannot carry on like this.'

The media camped on the Williams' doorstep in Wales for several days. There was analysis, debate, joy and dismay as everyone treated the *The Times* splash as almost an official announcement. *The Sun*, having heard that the family were fans of The Simpsons, arrived with a gift basket of every Simpsons trinket they could lay hands on – models, hats, pencils, videos, rulers. The bemused Primate was featured standing at his front door holding a box of Simpsons toys. He has since been invited to do a voiceover to feature in an episode.

'These were difficult months, to say the least, because we really didn't have a clue what was going on,' Williams says with a good deal of gratitude to Hope for his indefatigable support:

David was the only person who bothered to contact me during that time. He acknowledged that this would be a problem for Jane, myself and the two children and it helped me more than I can say. I really did have no idea what was going on. It was David's initiative to call. I immediately got a real sense of trust and support. And throughout that whole year, from the speculation to the appointment and the enthronement, David was consistently supportive.

The relationship between Williams and Hope was already very strong. Over years, Hope had developed a perfectly amicable relationship with George Carey, but it is now very clear that this was always going to be an exclusively working one. The two have hardly been in touch since Carey's retirement. Hope was given scant reference in Carey's aforementioned memoirs but George Carey is, nevertheless, positive about the time that he and Hope were Primates:

> It was an enormous pleasure to work with David as Archbishop of York. John Habgood was already in post when I went to Lambeth, and I enjoyed a good relationship with him too. But John is quite reserved and shy while David is a more open and naturally friendly type and we quickly established a good friendship. He was given a flat in Lambeth Palace for when he was working in London and, likewise, Eileen and I were always able to stay in a flat at Bishopthorpe when we were in the north of England. You don't do things like that if you are not good friends, do you?

Lord Carey is also positive about the advent of the Archbishop's Council, created to establish a beefed-up central administration, and acknowledges David Hope's great help in developing it. On one occasion, Hope referred to the new plethora of committees which resulted as Carey's Curia. Carey says:

> The changes which we made, and David was a big part of that process, pulled the Church of England together. While there are critics of the Archbishop's Council it has nevertheless given the Church a clear sense of being one, working together, pulling together. Bishop David has been very impressive in taking a lot of the load of administration in chairing various important groups and committees on behalf of the two archbishops, and I am full of admiration for him.

Most commentators agree that George Carey improved with experience in his post. David Hope would be the first to admit that he somehow managed to hold a very diverse set of people together and deal with complex issues. But Carey also presided over a huge drop in church attendances through what was supposed to be a Decade of Evangelism, and there was discernible disappointment among intellectuals that he had treated some issues with disdain. William Rees-Mogg wrote a scathing summary of the Carey years at Lambeth:

'Dr Carey has fought an honest battle – but his career has been at best a Christian Dunkirk, a noble retreat' (*The Times*, October 2002).

Ruth Gledhill understands how her front-page splash of Williams' appointment affected Hope. She even admits to 'not bothering him and keeping away for several months'. She smelt the anger, not directly from Hope but from the Church.

> Hope's relationship with Carey was a fascinating one but not one that got us in the media very excited. He and George Carey are very different. I don't think either of them would have picked the other as a best friend. But they did share a fundamental and straightforward faith from very different perspectives. As David got to know Carey more, he got to find out how he ticked and the relationship settled down after a difficult start in London. It was suggested to me after I had splashed Williams' appointment that Hope had been my source. That, because I have tried to work closely with Archbishop David, he was the only one who could have told me. But that, of course, was ridiculous. I now recognize that the Archbishop of York was furious when he heard the news and for a moment did not know what to do.
>
> We didn't communicate for a while. I felt for him as the only senior person left to deal with things. It was only afterwards, when all was officially confirmed, that the Archbishop of York made it clear to me that my splashing of the story could have robbed us of Rowan Williams at Canterbury. The prime minister could have gone for the second name.

Hope has his own thoughts as to who told *The Times*, and speculates about what their intentions might have been.

As Carey left and the nation waited to hear, officially, who was to succeed him, Hope set about keeping the show on the road. As well as his duties as Diocesan Bishop and Archbishop of the Northern Province, he had additional meetings in London and was in constant touch with senior staff at Lambeth Palace. He took it in his stride, presiding over the November sessions of the General Synod on his own and gaining a standing ovation for his care, diligence and oversight. By the following February, as Williams prepared for his enthronement in Canterbury Cathedral and with Britain on the brink of another war, as allies of the Americans, against Iraq, Hope began to see the end of a long episcopal tunnel. It would only be a matter of time after this new public ministry of Cantuar began that he could start to look forward to the rest of his life, and plans began to form.

He had a heavy few days presiding over his second General Synod without an Archbishop colleague. Williams turned up twice during the February sessions, once to be welcomed by the bishops, priests and laity at Church House and then, to the surprise of many, for an emergency debate on Iraq which both Primates had granted. Hope rose early in his Lambeth flat on the Monday, Tuesday and Wednesday mornings for prayer and mediation: by 7.30 he was in meetings which continued until after 11pm on all three days. On each of the days he sat alone in the archiepiscopal chairs staring out at the array of faces: colleagues, bishops, priests and laity. His patience with the Synod was wearing thin: 'It goes on endlessly,' he would say.

Rowan Williams is thankful for David's steady hand during those days. With the prospect of the war in Iraq growing all the time, Williams was certain that any armed conflict would be wrong, and he was grateful for David Hope's support when he made his first Synod appearance: 'We were very clear as archbishops what we wanted to say to the government and to the Church on Iraq at that point and there was a sense of unity of purpose and support.'

Prince Charles organized a dinner for George and Eileen Carey on the eve of Rowan Williams' enthronement. Hope was a guest at that dinner, returned to the Lambeth flat late at night and was on the road to Canterbury early on the Thursday morning. He took part in the rehearsal and enjoyed the enthronement. No one, apart from a few close friends, gave a thought to what was in the recesses of his mind that day. Immediately the ceremony was over, he dashed home. By 9pm he was in his armchair with a glass of wine reflecting on a frantic week – and on his future.

The fact that George Carey was Archbishop for a long period, covering Hope's time at London and York, had conspired to keep perhaps the finest Bishop in the Church of England from the top post. But he did not care at all about that. Rowan was in, and Hope was delighted. 'Now, let's get on with it,' he would say with more than a hint of relish. Hope has never doubted Williams, but has been concerned, at times, that all will be well for Rowan and his family.

Williams' admiration and gratitude that David Hope was at York is warm, genuine and refreshing: 'As a Welshman, I think I naturally resonate with a Yorkshireman! David has been an enormously strong colleague and I admire him greatly. What you see is what you get. That is refreshing. That mix of the undefended and the private. Great honesty and yet great reserve in the best possible way.'

In the autumn of 2002, Hope let it be known to Christopher Morgan of the *Sunday Times* that he had made up his mind to return to a parish well before the age of 70, the compulsory retirement age for an archbishop. Morgan was excited by the news: 'He really means it. He is going to go back to be a humble parish priest.' Hope could afford to enjoy the front-page story which followed which, in true *Sunday Times* fashion, reported that he was about to resign. The press office was deluged with calls. More enquiries came in about this story than any other in 2002. It was made clear to reporters that Hope had no intention of retiring in the foreseeable future but that he would like to return to a parish in due course. Lord Putnam of Queen's Gate said that the story had gone down extremely well and had done the Church no harm at all: 'After all, that is what the Church is all about: the parishes, the local church, and David has shown the people what counts,' he said.

Hope had calls the next day from flustered patrons and church-wardens offering him every kind of living imaginable. There were letters, faxes and e-mails offering him a job. Each day Hope was on his way to another living! But the nub of the story only added to the perception of Hope as a man of the people, a man increasingly frustrated by bureaucracy and meetings, a man who wanted to celebrate the sacraments and preach the word – openly, simply, in faith.

The build-up to conflict in the Gulf had developed a relentless momentum. Would Saddam Hussein do anything to avoid the seemingly inevitable war which President George W. Bush, supported by Tony Blair, was threatening? It seemed not. The whole thing depressed Hope: 'It is very serious. I can't remember a time when things seemed so serious, and they have got to sort the Holy Land out.' Hope was pressed again and again for his views on the possibility of armed conflict and steadfastly kept to the key point that he wanted to see a second United Nations resolution allowing the international community to deal with the Hussein regime and the question of weapons of mass destruction on a united front. The eventual rapprochement between the US/UK and France, Russia and Germany produced the grimmest of diplomatic scenarios.

Williams' opposition to conflict in the Gulf was well documented. He had been in New York, not far from the World Trade Center, on 11 September and understood American sensitivities, but he was clearly opposed to the use of force against Iraq. Although both wanted checks and balances in place, Hope was clearly more concerned that something should be done, something with the backing of international law to eradicate a regime which had lost all credibility. His various visits to the Middle East had confirmed in his own mind how degrading and undermining the regime of Saddam Hussein had become.

Hope's Easter Message in 2003 contained clear warnings to the allies about the future direction of foreign policy in the Gulf:

> Whatever one's views may have been or indeed continue to be about the war in Iraq, now that it has been engaged and the coalition forces are now more or less in control of the country, the top priority is surely the delivery of humanitarian aid where it is most needed, the regularizing of an interim administration, the restoration of a viable infrastructure – especially the supply of power and water – and all those things which go to make up a civil and democratic society, a task more easily spoken of than accomplished. And quite frankly, despite all the promises given, how things currently are in Kabul and Afghanistan post-war does not augur well as to how things might be in Baghdad and Iraq. At least as much determination, commitment, resolution will be needed on the part of the coalition which pursued the war now to pursue the construction.

When hostilities began, Hope issued a conservative statement:

> I am deeply troubled that the use of military force has today been undertaken in order to secure Iraq's compliance with the United Nations Security Council resolutions. The resort to war is always a sign of failure on the part of the international community. The thoughts and prayers of us all must be with those of our armed

forces currently involved in this conflict and for their families here at home – also for the chaplains and other support staff alongside them. The priority now must be for as speedy a resolution as possible of this crisis with minimum harm to the people of Iraq, and for putting in place such measures as will ensure a lasting justice and peace for Iraq and its long-suffering people.

In retrospect, Hope was too trusting of the Labour administration. Like many others, he believed in the accuracy of American and British intelligence as it was presented by the government, and it was not until several months later that the failure to find any weapons of mass destruction and the eruption of civil unrest across Iraq caused him to regret the support he had given.

Hope, of course, still had a diocese to attend to. He began the process of appointing a new Bishop of Selby and finding a new Dean of York as two of his senior team retired.

York Minster was a paradox to Hope. He loved it – the building, the history, the tradition, and the fact it was in Yorkshire. The reduction in the number of visitors due to 11 September, foot and mouth and now the Gulf War meant that the Minster simply could not balance its books. York would have to join St Paul's, Ely, Lincoln and Canterbury and charge for admission, hoping that the amount provided by its 1.3 million visitors each year would bridge the financial gap. The Cathedral needed £3.5 million per annum to keep it open and yet the average giving had been just over £1 per visitor. The Minster tried to coax tourists into giving a donation, but that simply did not work.

Hope was reluctant to make the move. 'I don't like it. I found the presence of the cash registers at St Paul's totally contrary to what a cathedral is or should be and I find the same response within myself at York Minster.' Advised that an announcement confirming charging was imminent after Easter 2003, Hope gave instructions that his displeasure should be made clear: 'I am deeply saddened by this news. Of course I understand the financial situation but I hope one day we can find a way of reversing this decision.' *The Times* suggested a new Trollope novel was on the horizon with the Archbishop and the Dean locked in conflict, but the Dean understood Hope's view and respected it.

Hope was regarded, by those concerned about the direction the Minster was taking, as the champion of tradition. After news that, in another cost-cutting measure, the Minster was thinking of removing the modern section (books from 1801 onwards) from the library and archives, the *Yorkshire Post* said: 'The Archbishop of York has emerged as the rallying point for protestors opposed to many of the Minster's current decisions. He may even invoke obscure sixth-century powers and use his visitatorial rights to enter the Minster, with a High Court judge and financial advisers in tow, to investigate its financial management.'

After years of urging by close friends to take more time in the Yorkshire Dales, it seemed that Hope was heeding their advice, eight years into the job at Bishopthorpe. He had bought a new house to the north of Skipton and managed to get there more often than to his old cottage. He also enjoyed getting to grips with the decoration and furnishing of his retreat. He chose a wonderful Yorkshire stone fireplace, set about buying some tasteful modern prints – nothing like the art which hung at Bishopthorpe – put an arch in the garden and had a lawn laid. Then he planned a conservatory. An infrequently used railway line lies close to Hope's home and he enjoys the odd train rumbling past. Sometimes, on bank holidays and Sundays, a steam train hurtles through, blowing its whistle, and he joins all the families at his fence to enjoy the great sight from the past. A less romantic sight is a succession of Virgin Voyager trains which are infrequently diverted past Hope's home: 'Oh yes, I have had quite a few Virgins past here today,' he trumpeted one Saturday as the third Birmingham express whizzed by.

There was a further overseas visit for Hope just after the Canterbury enthronement when he went on a five-day visit to Estonia to take part in a consultation with representatives of the Nordic Baltic churches. The Porvoo declaration marked a historic moment in ecumenical relations whereby the participant churches recognized each other as being in full communion. 'Church Leadership in a Changing World' was the theme of the visit: 'It was a time of real discussion as well as prayer and worship during which we were able to get to know each other even more.'

Hope planned two final pilgrimages, and made trips to Romania in 2003 and 2004. Hope's November 2003 visit was on behalf of

Children in Distress, seeing the work of the HIV/AIDS units working among children and encouraging the staff in their care for the patients. As he advances in years, Hope's love of Romania has become stronger. Stephen Platten, Bishop of Wakefield, remembers the enjoyment and commitment Hope displayed when he visited Romania with him several years before, and also the hilarity of the visit.

The City of Lasi is pronounced 'Yash' in English. We had to make an early morning dash to this ancient city in the east of Romania to meet the bishop there and visit a number of monasteries.

We left Bucharest fairly early and arrived in Lasi just before 7am. A splendid breakfast awaited us, but the first thing that we were offered was a slug of tuica. Tuica is home-made plum brandy and is a clear, colourless fluid which packs a good punch! David was slightly put off by such powerful liquor so early in the morning. 'Oh, we can't be doing with that this early in the day!' he said, and looked around for a suitable plant pot in which to pour the tuica, but before he had the chance the Bishop came into the room and greeted him with the equivalent of 'Your very good health' in Romanian. David had no choice but to knock back the liquor. The rest of the day seemed like a dream!

14

Steady in the Boat

> I think of David Hope as being steady in the boat. Like Jesus in
> the boat in the middle of a stormy sea. As the Church of England
> has torn itself apart over women priests and now over gays, what
> we have seen is calm pastoral leadership.
>
> (Christopher Morgan)

This portrait of David Hope has a consistency, a regularity to it. Such
consistency is partly what priesthood is about. Hope's days, structured
as they are within a framework of meditation and prayer, leave little
room for the unexpected. It is also a portrait of a life that has come
almost full circle. As I write, this former vicar is about to become
Vicar of St Margaret's Church, Ilkley. His sister Anne believes David
would have been a happy parish priest if that had been the total of his
ministry: 'He is more a man of the people than a man who likes committees and structures. An ordinary vicar in many ways. I can quite see
him as a vicar even now. Recently, we went to Thornes church where
our parents are buried and I watched him with people of all ages, just
chatting, being alongside them. That's what he likes most. Not all the
officialdom and so on.'

There is a sense that, in returning to parish ministry, Hope will
achieve a final fulfilment in a life that, because of the high offices he
has held, and the great and complex issues he has had to grapple with,
has not been as fulfilling as Hope might have wished. As this portrait
has shown, things have not been easy on the national and world stages
– and it is there that an Archbishop must act for much of his time. The
impasse in the Middle East, the Gulf War of 2003 that followed the

devastation wrought on New York, grave domestic issues such as foot
and mouth, the floods, and the rail disasters, mean that people have
lived through anxious times. Hope has risen well to the challenge of
helping us make our way through them. Quite whether, if pushed,
Hope believes that the Diocese of York has achieved all the things he
set out to tackle at the start of his ministry I am not sure, but there
have been many distractions and constraints – not least a significant
reduction in the number of stipendiary clergy available to do the
legwork in the parishes of the diocese. Hope is the first to admit that
this has been debilitating at times but that it has forced the Church to
look outwards to lay support and to give realistic attention to its
resources. Some of his friends remain concerned for him, anxious that
he will enjoy a significant enough retirement to unwind and find time
for himself.

In the last few years of his ministry, and certainly since the gay issue
affected the start of Rowan Williams' time at Lambeth in such a
dogged and persistent way, Hope's public utterances have been less
reserved and therefore more frank and radical. Christopher Morgan
of the *Sunday Times* acknowledges this and believes that Hope has
never realized the respect and authority he commands in the media:

> Editors like David Hope because he says it straight: they respect his
> view. It is considered and sane. I think of David Hope as being
> steady in the boat. Like Jesus in the boat in the middle of a stormy
> sea. As the Church of England has torn itself apart over women
> priests and now over gays, what we have seen is calm pastoral lead-
> ership. He has not been prone to issuing grand statements but has
> been perceived publicly and nationally as a good pastor.

We should also reflect on a quite radical sermon Hope delivered at
St Bartholomew's Church in Leeds on 3 March 2004, because it represents exactly where he stands on the one issue which has affected his
20 years in the House of Bishops. Hope spelt out, to both supporters
and opponents of women in the episcopate and women as priests, the
need for the Church to live together in its differences and not to tear
apart a body whose inherent task is to communicate communion,
wholeness and a sense of unity. This has always been his dilemma.
Hope does not believe that people should be pushed around because

of what they believe. Neither does he think that promises are made only to be broken. It was the tenth anniversary of the Act of Synod which reassured opponents of women's ordinations because it meant that it was as legitimate for them not to regard women as 'proper' priests, as to believe that they were. Now, however, some of those in favour of ordination were seeking to have the Act rescinded. Hope was forthright, clear and upbeat: 'It would be a tragedy if the Act of Synod were to be rescinded, it would be an act of betrayal and trigger a new crisis for our Church.' Hope had never been so clear. It was the kind of rhetoric opponents of women priests would have liked to have heard from him in his early years as Bishop of London. But it was almost as if he had gone as far as he could on this journey.

At the York Diocesan Clergy Conference in 2003, appreciation was given by delegates to the Archbishop. Not only for his pastoral care and support on a day to day basis, but for arranging a conference which had gone well and for the vision of 'Living the Gospel', the Mission Action Plan initiative.

A woman delegate begged permission of the Chair of the conference, the Bishop of Hull, to say a word. Assuming she just wanted to add her thanks, Bishop Richard urged her on. To his absolute horror the woman said that she wanted the Archbishop to know that many women in the diocese and province still felt alienated and ignored, and urged him to be more accepting. Hope's mind probably went back to the vicious comments made of him at Church House on the day of the vote by the two women deacons. There is an element within the 'For' lobby that still does not understand how opponents feel and, perhaps, why should they? In Leeds, Hope was clear that, in order to stay Anglican and in communion, such threatening behaviour, even intimidation, had to be put to one side and transformed: 'It will be important for all who are unable to accept the decision to ordain women to the ministerial priesthood for whatever reason to ensure open dialogue among bishops, priests and people so as to achieve some clear consensus about the way forward in respect of the ordination of women to the episcopate.'

The Catholic wing of the Church of England had offered a tremendous amount in the past and, though its future was uncertain, he was full of fervour: 'Be alert and alive to the many challenges and possibilities which today's world presents to communicate the

Christian life and faith in a lively and vibrant way.' That was his message and his hope. Over a thousand people packed the church to hear it. Stephen Bates interpreted this in the *Guardian* as a 'Crisis warning on women bishops'. Other newspapers followed the same line, praising Hope for his honesty and consistency. But it remains true that Hope has managed to remain much admired within the Catholic wing of the Church despite his reluctance to join any particular group or support any one cause. He has remained solid in his ministry as a Bishop within the Church of England and has been cautious in the extreme. Paradoxically, in playing his hand of cards thus, he has managed to ensure that the Catholic voice has been heard at the highest level within the Church and with a degree of respect and understanding which will be realized only when he has gone.

In an Ascension Day address, delivered at Pusey House in Oxford on 23 May 2004, Hope touched on many of the themes which have run through his ministry, and hence through this book. In what was likely to be one of his final major addresses, he delivered a wide-ranging and honest assessment of twenty-first-century Anglicanism. The address is suffused with Hope's guiding principles. He talks of the central importance of the One Holy Catholic and Apostolic Church, of which the Church of England must remain a part, of our Tractarian forebears who bequeathed the discipline of daily prayer, and of mission, which has always been at Hope's core.

Hope urged the Church to review and re-evaluate its effectiveness in mission and to be guided in this by the Holy Spirit.

> Just as the Lord was lifted up and a cloud took him out of their sight his very absence becomes a presence – a presence in the power of the Holy Spirit – that same spirit which fills the whole world. The moment of departure, the Lord's ascension, becomes the moment of mission. And it is the same Holy Spirit who guides and directs the mission of those 'churches the apostles left behind' as the biblical commentator Raymond Brown describes them.

The early Church was 'a spirit-filled, spirit-guided and spirit-led Church . . . a Church characterized by the gifts of the spirit so self-evident that as the Acts of the Apostles informs us "day by day the Lord added to their number those who were being saved". All of this is in sharp contrast to the state of the Church and the churches today.'

Modern society might be superficial, he went on, but it was

. . . a society which increasingly and paradoxically seems to be yearning for the things of the spirit – a yearning which apparently the churches are failing to satisfy. So what might be the nature of the mission entrusted to the Church in this twenty-first century?

In one sense of course it is none other than that which was entrusted to the first disciples – Go out into all the world . . . proclaim the kingdom . . . make disciples. The culture may have changed; the Church itself changed – the message remains the same. Jesus Christ the same yesterday, today and for ever. So the task of the Church, in one sense, is the same as ever it was – above all else, to remain faithful to the Lord who has called us and in baptism incorporated us into membership of his body the Church – the one Holy, Catholic and Apostolic Church.

We are called, I would suggest in the first place, to be faithful in worship – worship which certainly needs to be accessible yet at the same time awesome. The temptation, indeed the reality I experience in quite a number of churches, is simply to ape the passing styles of the times. Worship as entertainment; worship as distraction quite other than what it truly is or should be, namely the giving of worth to God. It is ironic that just at the time when not only so many young people but older people too have been captivated by the *Harry Potter/Lord of the Rings* genre of literature and film that the Church in its worship seems to have abandoned the mysterious in favour of the banal.

Our faithfulness in worship needs to be sustained by our faithfulness in prayer. It was our Tractarian forebears who restored to us and for us the discipline of daily prayer – a discipline without which . . . a prayer simply becomes a non-event.

A second dimension of our faithfulness is in teaching/learning/exploring the Christian faith and its implications and challenges for our living today.

There is a good deal around about the need for the Church to be a learning Church and one of the areas of 'learning' in particular, and not least in our theological colleges and courses for those preparing for ordination to the Sacred Ministry, is at the very least a basic knowledge of the early Church and the Fathers, as well as what I might describe as the Anglican tradition – what Michael Ramsey used to call 'theology with church bells'!

It's about being in touch with our roots, with our heritage, with our inheritance, with the Christian faith as the Church of England has received it.

We should remember 'our Tractarian forebears' who 'not only translated the ancient Fathers, they used them to great and converting effect in the Catholic renewal of this Church of England. There is an enormous challenge here to contemporary Anglicanism, not least given that we claim to be part of the one Holy, Catholic and Apostolic Church, that many of us and not least those preparing for ordination and those ordained need to become the more acquainted and familiar with this fundamental heritage and inheritance of our Church.'

We must also be faithful in witness: 'the most important witness which I believe is needed today more than ever, is the witness of "being" rather than "doing"', something of which Hope himself, in the way he has led his life and served his ministry, is a great example. 'Furthermore,' he continued, 'this "being" extends also to our style, manner and mode of living day by day.' It was in part about how people within the Church behaved towards each other. They should show, as those in the early Church did, 'kindness, gentleness, forbearance, long suffering and so on. Certainly, judging by the tone of some recent debates, they would be hard pushed to discern any such thing!'

When I asked Hope what he would like to be remembered for, he spoke of two things. One was the way in which he has striven to sustain the unity of the Church – something which he believes must be valued above all else. The other was the manner in which he has tried to do things, and the way he has sought to urge others to treat their fellows with courtesy and respect.

I have striven quite hard to try and ensure a courtesy of conversation between people of sharply different views for the sake of the Church in commending the Gospel for the world.

That has been at some considerable cost to myself at times, but I don't begrudge that at all. At times of dire threat to church unity I needed to do that to the maximum of my ability. Over the ordination of women to the priesthood, and again over the gay issue, which is dividing the Church, one has to use one's best efforts to seek to preserve the unity of the spirit and the bond of peace.

Everyone who has come across David Michael Hope has a story to tell. His humour. His bluntness. That facial expression and honesty. A sense that you were in the presence of someone who was marked out from the beginning to service the Church of God as a diligent pastor and teacher – without ever losing sight of the true meaning and purposes of it all. His time as Bishop of Wakefield will forever be remembered in his home town. His stint as Bishop of London will go down as an unfulfilled shaking of the very foundations of the structures of the Church in the most populous Diocese in the Church of England. And his time as Archbishop is regarded as a happy, confident and irreplaceable stint as leader of the Church in the north of England.

When the moment arrives and Hope retires as a stipendiary Bishop and Archbishop, he knows that he leaves the Church of England in the very capable hands of Rowan Williams. He is also aware of the clamour for an evangelical to succeed him, according to tradition, and his hope is for continuity and realism in his diocese and province. But when the Primatial Cross is handed over and the See of York is no longer in his care, the Archbishop of Canterbury is certain that Hope's massive contribution will not be forgotten: 'David's contribution has been enormous and we will miss him.'

Hope is probably looking forward to finding a little more of himself when he retires. He has had little time to do so up to now.

As he contemplates a life of great variety and controversy within a context of service and discipline, it is clear that these words of St Isaac the Syrian match his mood. He urged pilgrims at the end of their trip to Romania in March 2004 to live out these words on their earthly journey towards heaven. The room was silent as he said them. It was clear that they were his final charge:

Enter eagerly into the treasure house that lies within you, and so you will see the treasure house of heaven: for the two are the same, and there is but one single entry to them both. The ladder that leads to the Kingdom is hidden within you, and is found in your own soul. Dive into yourself and in your soul you will discover the rungs by which to ascend.

Index of Names